Reading in the content areas

An IRA Research Fund Monograph
in cooperation with the
ERIC Clearinghouse on Reading

**INTERNATIONAL
BOOK YEAR
1972**

UNESCO

Reading in the content areas

James L. Laffey
Series Editor
ERIC Clearinghouse on Reading

International Reading Association
Six Tyre Avenue   Newark, Delaware 19711
1972

372.4
L 163

ERIC/CRIER + IRA Monograph Series

James L. Laffey
Series Editor

Billie S. Strunk
Gail Kelly
Publications Editors

Trends and practices in secondary school reading: a review of the research

A. Sterl Artley (1968)

Reading diagnosis and remediation

Ruth Strang (1968)

Reading: what can be measured?

Roger Farr (1969)

Reading in the content areas

James L. Laffey, *Series Editor* (1972)

These monographs are available from the

International Reading Association
Six Tyre Avenue
Newark, Delaware 19711

Contents

Contributors

James L. Laffey
Indiana University

Donald R. Gallo
University of Colorado, Denver Center

Mary D. Siedow
Indiana University

Peter Hasselriis
University of Missouri — Columbia

Clyde G. Corle
The Pennsylvania State University

Myron L. Coulter
Western Michigan University

George G. Mallinson
Western Michigan University

Carl Bernard Smith
Indiana University

Thomas H. Estes
University of Virginia

Harold L. Herber
Syracuse University

Joseph T. Brennan
Duquesne University

James L. Laffey

Introduction

Reading in content subjects has been of interest to reading practitioners and scholars for more than four decades. One of the earliest attempts to explore ideas related to teaching content reading appeared in the *Yearbook of the National Society for the Study of Education* in 1925, and the search for answers to the issues has continued into subsequent decades. Most of the reported literature and textbooks have dealt primarily with questions related to practice. But more often than not, answers to practical questions were based on the considered opinions of authorities because very little research evidence existed regarding most of the questions raised by practitioners.

Therefore, the purpose of this monograph is twofold. First, it reviews, analyzes, and synthesizes where possible the findings of selected research related to content reading which has been conducted during the past two decades. Secondly, it describes how the findings of this research apply to classroom instruction.

There still aren't any simple answers to the complex questions related to what content reading research has contributed to classroom practice, but research in content reading has clearly demonstrated that a relationship does exist between skill in reading and success in content subjects (e.g., Artley, 1942). Some recent work reported by Herber and Sanders (1969) takes this relationship even further. Their findings offer evidence that student achievement is improved if the reading skills instruction is integrated with the content instruction. Although the evidence in the Herber and Sanders report is not scientifically overwhelming in favor of reading's contribution to subject matter learning, a major virtue of their work is that it builds a clear instructional rationale for conducting additional research in content reading. It suggests an hypothesis that can be tested: teaching reading skills instruction in the content area classroom provides a structure in which students can organize and apply their new knowledge to relevant materials in relevant situations.

This hypothesis relates to what Bruner calls the structure of knowledge. Bruner observes that:

> Knowledge is a model we construct to give meaning and structure to regularities in experience. The organizing ideas of any body of knowledge are inventions for rendering experience economical and connected. We invent concepts such as *force* in physics, the *bond* in chemistry, *motives* in psychology, *style* in literature as means to the end of comprehension. . . . The power of great organizing concepts is in large part that they permit us to understand and sometimes predict or change the world in which we live. But their power lies also in the fact that ideas provide instruments for experience. (p. 120)

The emphasis on structure which Bruner places on education generally is also an emphasis which reading specialists have attempted to place on reading. For example, Spache (1963) deals with one type of structure when he discusses the necessary foundational skills for reading in content areas, and he extends this structure even further by identifying seven general types of reading common to all content fields. He cautions, however, that "these [general types of reading] vary in emphasis in the various content fields . . . , but they include the basic skills needed for content reading." (p. 283)

While there are some shades of difference in *structure* as Bruner uses it and as it is discussed in the previous paragraph, the emphasis in both discussions is placed on constructing learning experiences so that there are regularities in experience. By applying Spache's two categories of reading skills—foundational skills and general reading skills—to learning in content subjects, it seems possible to regularize the reading experiences of students in content subjects. And by extending this structure to emphasize within each content classroom those skills that are most relevant to that content area, it seems possible to enhance student achievement.

However, if students are to benefit from the research findings which indicate that teaching relevant reading skills in content area classrooms is effective, teachers must know how to develop these skills as they apply to their specific subject areas. The first paper in each major section of this monograph is designed to review the research on the relationship between reading and success in a particular content area. Its purpose is to determine what is known and not known about teaching reading in the content classrooms of grades four through twelve, to identify problem areas, and to suggest areas in which additional research needs to be done.

The second paper in each major area is designed to use the research as a basis for offering practical suggestions about effectively developing the relevant reading skills. In cases where the research review revealed that much specific research still needs to be done, authors drew upon their professional expertise and experience to include practical suggestions for teaching obviously needed skills.

The emphasis of each section is on reading skills directly related to that content area rather than on general ones which overlap into all areas. Where general skills such as vocabulary acquisition have been treated by individual authors, the focus is on specific suggestions for developing the skill in their content area.

This approach does not deny the importance of these general skills, however; they too must be developed. They too have been the object of research studies. But it is the purpose of this monograph to deal primarily with those reading skills which will become the major responsibility of content area teachers, offering them ways to translate research findings into classroom practice.

References

Artley, A. S. A study of certain relationships existing between general reading comprehension and reading comprehension in a specific subject-matter area. *Journal of Educational Research,* 1944, *37,* 464-73.

Bruner, J. S. *On knowing.* Cambridge: Harvard University Press, 1962.

Herber, H. L. and Sanders, P. L. (Eds.) *Research in reading in the content area: first year report.* Syracuse, New York: Reading and Language Arts Center, Syracuse University, 1969.

Spache, G. Who is responsible for reading in the content fields? *Toward better reading,* Chapter 16, 273-97. Champaign, Illinois: Garrard Publishing Company, 1963.

Donald R. Gallo
Mary D. Siedow

Reading in literature:
The importance of student involvement

The teaching of reading implies careful attention to developing skill in word analysis, comprehension, and other areas so that facility in these skills will enable the reader to operate efficiently with printed material. But it must be remembered that these skills are tools and not ends in themselves. Children and adults usually do not read to see how many new words they can find, how many errors in logic a writer has made, or how often a particular figure of speech appears in a poem. Most reading is done for information or pleasure, and in reading literature the most important ingredient is involvement. The goal of a literature program, then, should be the interaction of book and reader to such a degree that ideas and emotions become paramount and reading skills become tools whose presence is unrealized.

It is the goal of this paper to point the way to such a program as it might exist in grades 4 through 12. The focus will be on encouraging students to become involved in reading so that reading can become an integral part of their lives. Considerably less attention will be paid to teaching reading skills as such. The first section of the paper contains a body of research dealing with individual involvement in literature and the effects of various forces on this involvement for young readers. The second section relates this research to the literature classroom, illustrating ways in which teachers can promote student involvement.

This particular treatment of the teaching of reading in the literature classroom assumes that the teacher is flexible in approach, actively involved in his own reading, and unruffled by demands for skill-oriented instruction. It also assumes that students can and will become involved in reading.

Research chosen for the monograph was selected for its applicability to the thesis. It reflects a larger sample of available research on reading in literature. Unfortunately, most of this research was conducted with populations of secondary students, frequently making it necessary to stretch the implications somewhat in order to refer to all students from grades 4 through 12. For the benefit of those who are interested in narrower grade level ranges, the grade levels of students involved are included in the discussions of various studies.

The elementary and secondary students whom this paper is ultimately intended to benefit are an interesting group. They are extremely involved in the goings-on of the world around them. Some of them find the world of school so far removed from the reality outside it that they are unable to cope with the disparities. Others attempt to compromise the two worlds and too often find that the compromise is the least relevant world of all. Some few refuse to become involved at all, as if involvement might force actions and emotions too difficult to control. The kind of program proposed here is geared to the removal of barriers between worlds. It is aimed at making school relevant to the outside world, not by compromise but by change of direction.

Today's young people are extremely well informed about the outside world. They get their information, at least in part, from the media bombardment they live in. Another part comes from interactions with parents, with other youth, and with schools. But these are by no means the only sources. The skeletal nature of TV and magazine coverage and the sometimes rambling, rarely conclusive nature of interpersonal communications do not allow sufficient exposure for formulating the kinds of deeply introspective opinions which youth has. There must be, and is, a further source helping to provide a solid base on which to build knowledge. That source, of course, is found in the numbers and types of books read by youth.

Reading habits of students: preferences and influences

Reading choices

Contrary to the often unchallenged accusation that young people no longer read voluntarily, studies of the reading habits of students in elementary and secondary schools show that these students do read outside of class. In fact, they read rather frequently and extensively. Using a questionnaire to survey reading activity in the month previous to receiving it, Squire and Applebee (1968) found that 16,089 senior high school students had obtained a total of 127,629 books either by buying them or by borrowing them from libraries, friends, or family. In another survey of reading habits, Gallo (1968a) discovered that on the day questionnaires were distributed to 262 eleventh graders from two suburban schools in central New York state, 47 per cent of the students were reading books of their own choosing outside of school. It is important to note that these students were not just the better students but represented all academic levels.

One big factor in the outside reading being done by so many students seems to be interest. Students want to know about a particular subject, or they have heard from friends that a particular book makes enjoyable reading. In an effort to determine the effects of interest on reading, Shnayer (1967) asked 252 boys and 232 girls from 17 West Coast sixth-grade classrooms to read 15 stories. The students were divided into seven ability groups and the stories they read were judged to have readability levels two grades higher than the students' abilities. The students rated their interest in the stories and were given comprehension quizzes when they finished. After comparing interest ratings and comprehension scores, Shnayer determined that a highly significant relationship existed between the two at all reading levels, but that this was particularly important at lower reading levels where students seemed to need interest to give them the motivation to continue despite difficulty.

Given the existence of a relationship between interest and reading, the next step toward involvement in reading is to find out what specific titles interest students. Whitman (1964) in a study of the questionnaire responses given by 975 students who were finalists in NCTE Achievement Awards programs in 1961, 1962, and 1963 found that about 416 titles were mentioned often enough to be of significance. Of these, 72 per cent were novels, 22.5 per cent nonfiction, and the rest poetry and drama. Of all the books listed, the 10 cited most frequently were *Catcher in the Rye; Exodus; The Ugly American; Crime and Punishment; Look Homeward, Angel; Of Human Bondage; Atlas Shrugged; Gone With the Wind; The Prophet;* and *Cry, the Beloved Country.*

In a later study which examined students of all achievement levels, Shirley (1968) found a somewhat different list of most frequently read books. The 430 Tucson, Arizona, high school students surveyed by Shirley chose the following titles as being influential in their lives: *Black Like Me, The Bible, To Kill a Mockingbird, Exodus, The Good Earth, Catcher in the Rye, The Ugly American, Animal Farm, Lord of the Flies,* and *The Grapes of Wrath.*

Both the Squire and Applebee (1968) and the Gallo (1968a) studies of student reading gave lists of frequently read titles. Again there are differences between the lists, but there are also some interesting similarities. The Squire and Applebee study listed these top 10 books: *Lord of the Flies, Catcher in the Rye, To Kill a Mockingbird, 1984, The Bible, Crime and Punishment, Gone With the Wind, The Robe, Black Like Me,* and *Cry, the Beloved Country.* The Gallo study listed these four titles: *Gone With the Wind, Catcher in the Rye, 1984,* and *To Kill a Mockingbird* as being the most frequently cited in a survey to determine the "best" book ever read by respondents.

Two particularly significant observations may be made after examining these studies. One is that certain books appear over and over again, indicating that books like *Catcher in the Rye,*

To Kill a Mockingbird, and *Cry, the Beloved Country* have something to say to the majority of today's youth. The other observation is that only a relatively small percentage of students choose the same title when asked for a single "best" or most influential book. The implication seems clear that individuals respond differently to the same materials.

The varying responses of individuals seem certain to be based on the differences existing among those individuals, for each person has needs, desires, likes, and dislikes of his own. Some of these may be dependent upon his age or sex, some on other factors. There are some needs, some influences, which seem to affect most readers, however, and these are worthy of consideration here.

Reading influences

A study conducted in Japan by Sakamoto, Hayashi, and Kamei (1967) illustrates the factors which are likely to influence students' reading habits. In their study of 3,000 book reports written by students ranging in age from primary to secondary levels, the authors found personal, social, and cultural factors in addition to the age and sex factors they had expected. Personal problems were most frequent among very young students, social problems among junior high school students, and cultural problems among high school students. Boys were most interested in "scientific attitudes" and "attitudes toward others," while girls were interested in "forming one's view of life" and "affection." The previously mentioned study by Shirley (1968) also showed that self-image, involvement, social and cultural problems, and philosophy of life were important factors in reading interest. One might easily expect that a fourth area, environmental factors, could be added to the personal, social, and cultural factors noted in these studies. One might further expect that, while certain factors are of primary importance at one age, they are present but relegated to background positions at other ages.

Personal influences. A considerable number of studies have

5

been conducted on the personal involvement of the individual with his reading. Most of them have identified self-involvement, role identification, self-image, attitudes and values, and developmental tasks as major personal influences. Squire's (1964) study of the responses of 52 ninth and tenth graders while reading four short stories is one of the best known of these. In this study, Squire divided each story into sections and interviewed students as they completed the reading of the section. Analysis of their responses identified seven categories of response, including self-involvement. As a result of these responses, Squire concluded that readers who were self involved were superior readers in that they opened themselves to a maximum of facets and accommodated imaginatively the widest possible number of avenues to literary experience. In short, their literary judgment seemed directly correlated to their self-involvement.

Wilson (1966) asked 54 college freshmen to read three novels, write notes while reading, write their immediate reactions after reading, and write followup reactions after discussion. The written responses to *Catcher in the Rye, Gone With the Wind,* and *A Farewell to Arms* were then coded according to Squire's (1964) categories and analyzed. Wilson concluded that initial self-involvement seems necessary if students are to make effective interpretations. His subjects seemed to flounder at the beginning of a novel, but their interpretations became more formulated and their insights became more meaningful as time passed and class discussions were held. As their involvement with the work became greater, so did their ability to analyze and discuss it.

The relationship of an individual's concept of his role in a society to his self-involvement with reading is a subject of great interest, particularly to groups for whom role identification is important. Barrett and Barrett (1966) sought to determine the relationship between enjoyment of stories and role identification by presenting three stories to 40 Negro fourth graders in an urban school. The children read the stories in random order and then stated a preference for one of them. Seven children selected the story about a white boy who lived in a pleasant country home, and three chose the story about a boy who lived in a foreign country. The remaining children all chose the story about a Negro boy living in an urban environment.

An aspect of personal involvement closely related to role identification is self-image. In his study, Shirley (1968) determined that the books which were most influential in the lives of readers were those which affected self-image. In another previously mentioned study, Whitman (1964) investigated the choices of books identified as significant by superior English students. The principal reason given for this designation was that the books in some way helped shape the readers' attitudes, values, or thoughts.

At the preadolescent level, some factors may assume an importance which they do not have for older students. Worley (1967) examined stories read by 1,500 fifth and sixth graders and identified developmental tasks with which they were concerned. Five personal-social types of developmental tasks emerged as being of great importance: 1] achieving a dependence-independence pattern, 2] achieving a giving-receiving pattern of affection, 3] relating with social groups, 4] developing a conscience and morality, and 5] learning one's psycho-social sex role.

What all of these studies have shown is that personal involvement in subject matter or theme is a strong influence on reading. Such an influence is so strong, in fact, that it deserves to play a central role in the design of any literature program.

Social, cultural, and environmental influences. The social and cultural interests outlined in the Sakamoto, Hayashi, and Kamei (1967) study appear to be borne out in the several studies mentioned previously in which specific titles were listed. Even casual observation shows the preponderance of books with social themes: *Cry, the Beloved Country; Exodus;* and *Animal Farm,* for example. Surely the interest of young people in their society is evident not only in their reading but also in their sincere and often outspoken involvement in current political and social issues.

The effects of environment on reading interests are more difficult to measure because of the often contradictory results of studies in this area. It seems logical that an individual's environment should somehow affect his reading habits and interests, but the exact direction of the effect is open to question. In a study already described, Barrett and Barrett (1966) found that inner-city Negro children preferred stories about children like themselves to those about suburban white children. In another study, however, the opposite was found to be the case. Emans (1968) selected 12 stories from first-grade reading programs, six with multiethnic-city themes and six with family-friends-pets themes. These stories were read to 22 inner-city children, 11 boys and 11 girls, none of whom had yet started formal reading programs. While some children preferred the multiethnic stories, the majority preferred the family-friends-pets themes. This preference showed up again in a replication using 14 boys and 10 girls in another inner-city school. The seeming incompatibility of the findings of the Barrett and Barrett and the Emans studies is indicative of the need for further research with the effects of environment. It is also indicative of the number of factors which may influence an individual's preferences, making prediction of those preferences difficult indeed.

It may be that the influence of environment does not unswervingly follow socioeconomic lines. Certainly the number of culture- and environment-related titles cited in the preference studies is indicative of an interest in expanding intellectual boundaries on the subject. This seems to have been the case with the middle class suburban youth who were surveyed for the studies.

As for the youth of less advantaged environments, perhaps the most revealing work done on their reading is that of Fader and McNeil (1968). One of the results of Fader's saturation reading program is an indication that, while they have greater difficulty in reading, disadvantaged youth are as interested in becoming personally involved in reading as are middle class youth. Personal development, role identification, and attitude formation are vitally important and lead to sociocultural interests as keen as those of their middle class counterparts. A look at Fader's list of recommended books points this out clearly and suggests the possible hypothesis that the big difference between reading interests of low- and middle-socioeconomic groups is one of degree and not of kind, with the low groups following a few years behind in personal, social, and cultural interests.

Types of available books. A third major influence on the reading habits of youth is the availability of certain types of books. A quick look at typical school syllabi and at the results of the surveys of reading interests described above shows how little overlap exists between what students read in school and outside of it. Whitworth's (1964) survey of high school seniors in Indianapolis indicated that students expressed a desire to read but that most of these students read different books in and out of school. A major reason given for the difference in choice of materials was that materials available in public libraries and bookstores were different from those available in classrooms. Such a difference is revealing when considered in the light of teachers' stated efforts to promote student interest in reading by providing relevant materials.

Perhaps a more revealing aspect of outside reading is that so many of the books commonly named by students in surveys are, or were at one time, controversial in nature. Whitman (1964) commented on this, noting that the most commonly cited book in his study, *Catcher in the Rye,* has also been a most controversial book for some time. Further indication of the influence of controversial titles on reading habits was found by Shirley (1968) who quoted a student as saying that these preferred books are too controversial for school libraries and that students, therefore, either miss a good deal of valuable reading or seek outside sources of supply. It is interesting to note that Squire and Applebee (1968) found *Catcher in the Rye* in only 50 per cent of the school libraries they surveyed.

Finally, there is the indication that even the binding process used in printing a book influences the extent to which it is read by youth. The availability of paperback books encourages reading. Lowery and Grafft (1968) encouraged fourth graders to read independently and provided them with the same 40 titles in hard cover and in paperback. Those groups given paperbacks read more and showed significant gains in positive attitudes over the hard cover groups. Lowery and Grafft speculated that size, attractive covers, handling ease, and lack of association with previous scholastic failure might be influences at work here. These seem to be factors enmeshed in the reading process that cannot be ignored.

Readability level. To this point, comments have been made regarding the content of reading materials: whether or not students find the stories interesting to them, whether the content is related to their personal and social needs, and whether the cultural biases apply to them. Each of these has been examined in relative isolation, but when they are examined together, something slightly different occurs. As a unit, these factors constitute a part of any book's readability level. In the total picture, a major question in reading literature, or anything else for that matter, is "How readable is it?"

The content of literature curricula as related to readability was studied by Corbin and Crosby (1965). They reported that secondary schools tend to emphasize nonliterary reading materials such as workbooks and reading exercises, or they use anthologies whose contents bear little relation to the capabilities and interests of students, particularly of disadvantaged students.

Yet content alone does not determine readability. Other aspects of a book's readability level are its linguistic and stylistic complexities. Aukerman (1965) developed a device for measuring readability consisting of mechanical and verbal complexity factors. When he applied his device to 66 secondary school literature anthologies, he found great variations among and within them on both sets of factors. Few, if any, of the anthologies could be read independently by the underachieving reader. Therefore, he estimated that at least 3,000,000 students in the United States cannot read their assigned texts.

From reports such as these, it seems obvious that there is

much to be done in relating the difficulty levels of materials to the interests of students. Further research into readability formulas and further attention to student interest in selecting materials are quite obviously called for. Until students can pursue their interests through books they can read, there seems very little likelihood that school literature programs will increase their successfulness.

Mass media. While individuals often do pursue their interests through books, these interests are influenced by what the individuals see and hear daily through the mass media. The effects of mass media on reading habits have been the subject of a vast quantity of study and opinion. Certainly it must be stated that the mass media world of newspapers, magazines, television, and movies is a real and vital part of present day living. Since today's school-age population appears to be more visually than verbally oriented, the study of film and "media" has become increasingly more important as part of the language arts program or as a separate class in itself. Many educators as well as parents have been concerned about the influence of these media on the reading habits and skills of youngsters. In general, the recent research examined for this paper indicates that there is no detrimental effect of television and films on students' reading. In fact, the very opposite may be true.

One study which supports such a conclusion is that of Loughlin and Loughlin (1968). Their comparison of reading achievement and TV viewing habits of intermediate-grade children showed no significant difference in TV viewing for good and poor readers. Witty's (1966) survey of television use over a 15-year period showed that approximately one-half of the elementary students surveyed felt TV actually helped them in school, and one-fourth felt that TV also influenced their reading of books. At the high school level, the favorable effect of media on the reading of juniors can be seen in Gallo's (1968a) survey in which 62 per cent of the respondents were motivated to read books by having seen movies adapted from them.

How schools can affect student reading habits

Given the above information on the importance of personal involvement and interest, what approaches would schools use? How can schools affect what is read by students? It seems probable that several ways have already presented themselves to the reader. If so, the reader will agree that implications of the reported research are clear and far reaching. He will also agree that, while some of the possible means of affecting student reading are novel and complex, others are obvious and simple to employ.

Perhaps the most significant fact in favor of schools is that students do read many books, newspapers, and magazines that are not assigned material. What is needed is to find ways to utilize that reading, to channel the school program into the interests of the students. Doing this demands considerable restructuring of a teacher's values regarding the content, relevance, and methodology of what he teaches.

Within the confines of the literature program lie both the most fertile possibilities for change and the most fervid reaction against it. At the one extreme is the traditional anthology-plus-novel-plus-one-Shakespearean-play approach to each year of the high school English curriculum. At the other is the freely structured, highly individualized approach of far too few brave experimenters. Between the extremes are teachers whose programs reflect varying degrees of balance between the traditional and the experimental. The suggestions which follow are based on general conclusions reached through study of the literature reported above and are intended for teachers of all kinds of programs.

The research reported above stresses the desire of young readers to involve themselves in their reading. Both Squire (1964) and Wilson (1966) made special note of the importance of the role of self-involvement in a student's understanding and analysis of a literary work. Barrett and Barrett (1966) showed how strong the need to identify one's role can be, and Shirley (1968) pointed to a need to develop self-image as a motivational factor in reading. The use of books in formulating attitudes and values was noted by Whitman (1964), and the possibilities for devising developmental tasks from book subjects were suggested by Worley (1967).

Instructional methods

Translating the notion of self-involvement into classroom procedure can take a number of paths. One of these might be the use of a "self-concept" unit such as those contained in many written curricula or in commercially packaged units. Teachers might study these as possible sources of ideas and as possible starting points for book selection.

Another method might be frequent free reading time in class. Teachers can use the time to find out what books are of interest to the students, to make observations of students' reading habits (and possibly of their reading levels), to interact with students on points of mutual interest, to provide assistance on an individual basis, and to identify topics for further class study. Students can use the time to further their interests in various topics, to share these interests with classmates and teachers, and to simply enjoy the luxury of uninterrupted reading time. Skillful use of free reading time should allow for all of this: for sharing, for instruction, and for leisure.

The journal is a third possible classroom procedure which has proved to be popular with teachers and students for more obvious reasons than it is necessary to relate here. In the literature classroom it can provide a place for students to react to their reading on a personal level which might otherwise be impossible. It may eventually evolve into an intimate two-way communication device between student and teacher, although this is not its primary purpose. The journal can also become a vehicle for personal expression through which students may find creative abilities of which they were previously unaware. In the first weeks of journal use, frequent checking by teachers may be necessary to insure student writing. After that, checking may slow down to allow greater freedom of expression while assuring teacher interest.

Another possibility is the introduction of controversial topics in class. Such subject matter is vital to a relevant literature program. Neither teacher nor students should feel constraint about whether such topics belong in classrooms, since there is probably no more constantly available, relaxed atmosphere for the interaction and guidance necessary to such discussion.

Discussion of a controversial topic might be begun by the teacher as a preview of a TV presentation on the topic or as an individual reaction to a newspaper editorial. Students might take the initiative by mentioning some item of contention within the school or by asking the class's viewpoint on issues around which the plot of a movie is formed. If the classroom atmosphere is free from arbitrary restraint, mutual trust can build a camaraderie which will allow increased and continued consideration of whatever issues and problems are currently in the minds of students. References to titles of related books may be made, and reading these books as outgrowths of discussion can, in turn, influence further discussion.

A final possibility, especially for teachers of disadvantaged students, is to fill the classroom with reading materials from which they can choose freely. The Fader (1968) program, and others which have appeared in popular literature, involved disadvantaged students in successful programs of individualized reading with free choice of materials. Carleton and Moore (1966) allowed elementary school children to choose stories to read and to choose characters and situations from the stories to dramatize. After the 3½-month experiment, these children showed significantly greater gains in reading achievement than did control groups.

Regardless of methods used in the classroom, a major factor in program success is teacher enthusiasm for and interest in reading. One way to communicate these qualities is for teachers to carry the books (especially paperbacks) they are currently reading, leaving them conspicuously on desks for students to see and to comment on. Periodically teachers could also browse through the paperback selections in stores near the school, perhaps suggesting titles to the proprietors and reporting available books to students.

Materials

Content.   It is all too often the case that teachers must use whatever materials are made available to them or do without.   But it is equally true that too many teachers show little or no imagination in their utilization of materials.   The teacher who depends solely on an anthology because class sets are assigned to him is missing a great many opportunities at his disposal, to say nothing of running the risk of losing his students because they do not find relevance in anthology selections.   Squire and Applebee (1968) commented on the preference of young people for contemporary works as opposed to the classical selections usually found in schools.   Blount (1965) found junior novels to be highly effective for teaching the novel form. His results indicated that the junior novels (*The Sea Gulls Woke Me, Street Rod,* and *Swiftwater)* were as effective as the adult novels (*Ivanhoe, Red Badge of Courage,* and *Silas Marner)* in bringing ninth- and tenth-grade students to a mature concept of the ideal novel. This effectiveness was noted for boys as well as girls at both age levels. These findings suggest that teachers need to reevaluate their reasons for not using junior novels.   If students are interested in these novels, there seems little justification for excluding them from classrooms on grounds such as lack of literary merit, an often-cited excuse. Blount's findings are underscored by the recommendations of Petitt (1963) who provides ideas for using specific junior novels and by Nelms (1966) who presents a plan which includes junior novels in a threefold program involving books for browsing, for fun, and for analysis and discussion.

Materials types and sources.   Yet relevant subject matter alone does not completely solve the materials problem.   Individualized programs require quantities of materials. Squire and Applebee (1968) noted that two conferences of high school department chairmen recommended libraries of approximately 500 titles in every English classroom. Obviously such a library is needed; obviously the cost is high. Evidence repeatedly suggests that the solution is paperback books. Their abundance, their low cost, and their wide range of subject matter are advantages no classroom teacher can afford to overlook. Their small size, the ease with which they can be handled, carried, even hidden and replaced, are advantages which appeal to students. The fact that extremely successful programs have been built around paperback books serves as proof of their effectiveness. Fink and Bogart (1965) reported that the use and accessibility of paperbacks in classrooms can effect desirable changes in students at all grade levels. Fader and McNeil's (1968) program of saturating classrooms with paperback reading materials met with greater success than anyone had predicted. (Particular reference is made to these reports so that teachers can consult them for specific information about their workings.)

Teachers who avoid the anthology-only approach in an effort to provide relevant subject matter and to offer a wide variety of reading choices might well use the anthology as a resource. This might mean recommending selections relevant to topics of student interest and fitting some, but not all, of the selections into units on topics resulting from student interest.

In addition to the anthology selections, teachers might use novels, short stories, biographies, etc. (many of them paperbacks) which students suggest. Even when emphasis is to be placed on one theme, it probably does not matter whether everyone reads the same book as long as each book deals with the selected theme—a theme, of course, which students find worth discussing. Teachers reticent to try the many-book approach are reminded that rarely is an assignment read by 100 per cent of the students anyway, so rarely is an entire class able to discuss even one book. In discussing a particular literary form, it may even be advantageous if several different books have been read. Then contrast can be introduced to show how the form is adapted to the needs of the subject.

A fertile classroom materials source which must not be overlooked is the junior novel. This genre often appears in paperback and deserves scrutiny by teachers, especially by teachers with vague memories of boy-meets-girl novels from their own youths. Today's junior novels deal with an unbelievable range of relevant subjects and are usually written in excellent literary style, making them almost certain hits with intermediate, junior high, and even some senior high students. Teachers would be well advised to inject junior novels into their personal reading schedules so that familiarity with them might offer a new avenue of approach to students. Many teachers report that students are happy to find them reading these books and that new communications are opened when teachers show a personal interest in junior novels and short stories.

As noted earlier, a major factor in any literature program is quantity of materials. If paperbacks are not made available by the school and if no benefactor such as Fader's (1968) can be found, other solutions must be sought. One alternative might be to join classroom book clubs. Students can select books for their own personal libraries and/or for a classroom collection. Another solution might be an occasional book trading day. This offers students an opportunity to share their feelings about books and to trade books with other students. Perhaps this activity can be an adjunct to a free reading period. Finally, books on topics being studied in class may be borrowed from the school library. Teachers may want to recommend the best of these and let students share their opinions of them.

However, materials need not be limited to books. Magazines and newspapers can be introduced into the materials available to the class. Periodic visits to the library will keep teachers familiar with current magazines of interest to children, teenagers, and adults so that the magazines or topics considered in them can be brought to the attention of their students.

Readability level. Regardless of how interested or involved they may be in a specific story or problem, young people will have difficulty reading material which is written at a level far beyond their abilities. Difficulty in reading can be so frustrating to a youthful reader that it may discourage him altogether.

Teachers have means at their disposal to prevent such frustrating experiences. Readability formulas can be used to determine the difficulty level of books and other materials. Research has already been cited which indicates that many of the materials found in school literature curricula are written at levels far too difficult for average and below-average readers (Aukerman, 1965; Corbin and Crosby, 1965). While the formulas they used are perhaps too complex to be useful to the classroom teacher, other formulas are available. The Spache and Dale-Chall formulas, which are based on word count, have been used for many years. Although there is considerable discussion currently as to their validity, and although they involve time-consuming processes, these formulas should give teachers sufficient information about difficulty levels to be useful in counseling students. A similar readability formula, SMOG, is also based on word count; however, it is a less time-consuming and more accurate process than the others because it has a less-complicated structure and because it indicates the grade level which a reader must have attained in order to fully comprehend the text (McLaughlin, 1969). Other approaches to readability assessment include the cloze procedure which involves word deletion rather than word count. Bormuth's (1963, 1965, 1966) experiments with this process have produced new and efficient ways to judge readability.

Whatever the means selected, readability formulas are usually complex and require considerable application time. Teachers, therefore, would be well advised to enlist the aid of fellow teachers and school librarians in using readability formulas. Some better readers at the senior high school level might also be recruited to help with the task. By making sure that the materials examined for difficulty contain varied samples from many subjects, teachers can get some direction in guiding students to books they can both read and enjoy.

If all else fails, teachers can rely to some extent on their own observations of students' reading for indications of whether material is too difficult. Students who seem uncomfortable with books or who are unable to coherently relate the story they are reading might be greatly helped by referring them to other available and less-frustrating materials.

Mass media. Even if continual frustration has kept some young people from books, most of them have kept abreast of the ideas and themes developed through the mass media. Nearly everyone watches TV and goes to movies. Radios are carried to almost every place people go. The influence of these and other media continues to increase in frequency and in effect. Loughlin and Loughlin's (1968) research showed that good and poor readers watch equal amounts of TV, and Gallo's (1968a) study showed that TV and movie viewing can induce students to read books. Witty's (1966) study indicated that many children feel they are aided in school work by TV and movie viewing.

If media impact is this great, the media must surely be incorporated into classroom practice. It must be considered a classroom material. Schools are beginning to install their own closed-circuit TV systems so that experiments in media use can be conducted. Movies and records have been in use for some time. Some effort has been made to relate commercial TV offerings to curricula. Weekly classroom magazines received by students often contain study guides related to upcoming TV shows, and sponsors of some TV specials make similar study guides available to schools. In addition, scenarios from movies, television programs, and stage plays are frequently found in magazines for students such as *Scope, Read,* and *Literary Cavalcade.* Many teachers—especially those with less capable students—have had tremendous success in motivating and improving reading skills through the use of these magazines.

All of this is to be encouraged. In a saturation reading program, everything which touches a student is important. The most obvious way of capitalizing on media offerings is to pair books with the movies or TV shows adapted from them. And, since movies and TV shows are often concerned with the same themes being read and discussed in class, this direct pairing can be expanded to an open policy for discussing any recent and upcoming shows which are related. Other methods of media utilization also exist. For example, critical reading techniques can be extended to daily and special news broadcasts. The important factors to consider in the classroom use of mass media are awareness and timing. Teachers must keep alert to upcoming media presentations and must be flexible enough in their planning to schedule reading assignments accordingly and to allow even unexpected shows to be discussed in class.

Instructional practices

The importance of instructional practices to the success of a program cannot be overemphasized. What teachers do in classrooms greatly affects the learning that takes place there. The aim of this paper has been to advocate a free classroom in which students have maximum opportunities to learn. Within the literature program, this has meant providing students with freedom and with the materials and guidance to read widely and well. Some general ideas for instructional methods suitable to the aim have already been discussed. In this final section, research on specific instructional practices will be described.

The structure of assignments has been shown to affect their successfulness. Smith (1968) hypothesized that preassigned creative writing tasks would establish purposes for reading and would thus result in better reading habits. Although results of his experiment with high school seniors showed that positive attitudes were not fostered by assigning creative writing tasks before reading, he did find that the specific type of assignment made a difference, since students assigned noncreative tasks showed improved attitudes.

In a provocative recent study, Guszak (1967) examined the effects of teacher questioning styles on second, fourth, and sixth graders. Reading groups in selected classes were observed for five hours each over a three-day period. From the analysis, Guszak found that 70 per cent of the questions asked were recall questions concerned only with the most obvious factual details of the stories. Students appeared to expect such questions, according to Guszak, and were prepared to answer them correctly on the first try 90 per cent of the time.

A similar study specifically related to poetry was done by Gallo (1968b). He observed the practices used in presenting poems and found that the methods used varied little. Teachers tended to either read a poem aloud, or have a student read it without previous study, and then tended to ask factual questions about the poetic devices used, the meanings of specific lines, and the poet's biography.

When these two studies are considered together, the implications they have for instructional practices are extremely clear. The questions used in the first study led children to expect nothing beyond memory of simple facts. They gave up trying to find any meaning beyond details, if indeed they had ever looked for such meaning. Unless instructional practices used are somehow changed, children will grow up thinking that reading is nothing more than finding facts and that literature is nothing more than a place to find them.

If poor questioning techniques are undesirable in prose, they are deadly in poetry. Basically poetry is to be reacted to, and that is the way most adults want to read it. The poetic devices serve the poet as means to his end, and they should be studied as means, not as the primary focus of classroom discussions of poetry. Surely every teacher has had a student say, "But I just don't feel that way about this poem!" Perhaps feeling is the place to start, allowing students free rein to express the ways in which they have reacted to the poem. There is plenty of time later to determine how the poet made those feelings happen.

One way of avoiding the rote classroom activity found by Guszak (1967) and Gallo (1968b) in their studies is the open class, free choice program proposed here. Bogart (1966) reported an interesting program using the free choice paperback approach. In the program, elementary and secondary students from 50 New Jersey schools were allowed to order books from 45 members of the American Book Publishers Council. Over 8,000 students participated in the program, ordering over

40,000 books. Once they had the books, students read them, discussed them, and traded them. The result was student involvement, the very aim toward which this paper has been directed. Both students and teachers felt that the program was beneficial and rewarding and that it should be continued as a replacement for previous curricula.

Even with all this proposed freedom in classrooms, there often is still a need for some kind of structure to guide activity. But structures need not mean anthology-shackled daily lesson plans. Instead, teachers attuned to student interests can propose thematic units based on subjects in which students are or wish to be involved. Bogart's (1966) study utilized thematic units in that student reading choices were structured around broad subjects which could act as a focal point for classroom discussion. Within the individualized thematic unit, there was opportunity for reading and discussing all forms of literature without the constraints of technical form or reading level.

A final point to be remembered in constructing a free reading curriculum is that for it to be effective there must be interaction between classroom and free time. The class period must cease to be a time for only lecture and discussion and begin to include time for reading. McCracken (1969) proposes that in-class time be allotted for sustained silent reading. Students should be allowed to choose reading material and then to read that material for a designated amount of time, perhaps 30 minutes every day. The idea is based on the premise that students deem important what the school makes obvious it considers important. If a teacher spends most of his time talking about reading, taking attendance, and collecting money for yearbook pictures, students will infer that these are considered important by the teacher. If, on the other hand, a teacher sits down with the students at regular intervals and reads and if he provides an opportunity for them to choose from a large selection of materials, then reading will appear important. Sustained silent reading should become part of every school's program.

The research described in this paper and the ideas for adapting that research for classroom use should combine to make a successful literature program. Teachers hoping to use the ideas should keep several things in mind. First of all, the research, while sometimes containing contradictory evidence, presents a reasonably clear case for teaching to the interests of students and points specifically to interests which can be used in classes. Second, most of the ideas given had been successfully used in programs before coming to the attention of the writers. There seems little doubt that they can work again. Third, if some ideas appear to have been repeated too frequently already, it may be the case that teachers have not been willing to try them; consequently, they are still experimental in nature.

Unfortunately, it is impossible to offer a money-back guarantee that any program will be completely successful. It is possible, however, to state that the premises on which the proposed program is based are sound, that many of the ideas it includes have been proved successful, and that the research done both on premises and ideas has shown successes in both areas. Given skillful teaching, there seems little reason to assume that success will not result from full scale application of the program.

References

Aukerman, R. C. Readability of secondary school literature textbooks: a first report. *English Journal*, 1965, *54*, 533-40.

Barrett, C. Patricia and Barrett, G. V. Enjoyment of stories in terms of role identification. *Perceptual and Motor Skills*, 1966, *23*, 1164.

Blount, N. S. The effect of selected junior novels and selected adult novels on student attitudes toward the "ideal" novel. *The Journal of Educational Research*, 1965, *59* (4), 179-82.

Bogart, M. Paperback books in New Jersey. In Vivienne Anderson (Ed.), *Paperbacks in Education*. New York: Teachers College Press, Teachers College, Columbia University, 1966.

Bormuth, J. R. Cloze as a measure of readability. In J. A. Figurel (Ed.), Reading as an intellectual activity. *Proceedings of the International Reading Association*, 1963, *8*, 131-34.

Bormuth, J. R. Optimum sample size and cloze test length in readability measurement. *Journal of Educational Measurement*, 1965, *2*, 111-16.

Bormuth, J. R. Readability: a new approach. *Reading Research Quarterly*, 1966, *1* (3), 5-34.

Carlton, Lessie, and Moore, R. H. The effects of self-directive dramatization on reading achievement and self-concept of culturally disadvantaged children. *The Reading Teacher*, 1966, *20*, 125-30.

Corbin, R., and Crosby, Muriel. (Eds.) *Language programs for the disadvantaged*. Champaign, Ill.: National Council of Teachers of English, 1965.

Emans, R. What do children in the inner city like to read? *Elementary English*, 1968, *69*, 118-22.

Fader, D. N., and McNeil, E. B. *Hooked on books: program and proof*. New York: Putnam and Sons, 1968.

Fink, R., and Bogart, M. *Paperbound books in New Jersey public schools*. Trenton, N. J.: State Department of Education, 1965.

Gallo, D. R. Free reading and book reports—an informal survey of grade eleven. *Journal of Reading*, 1968, *11*, 532-38. (a)

Gallo, D. R. The construction and validation of an instrument to assess teachers' opinions of methods of teaching poetry to tenth grade students of average ability. Unpublished doctoral dissertation, Syracuse University, 1968. (b)

Guszak, F. J. Teacher questioning and reading. *The Reading Teacher,* 1967, *21,* 227-34.

Loughlin, Emma C., and Loughlin, L. J. A study of the relationship of time spent viewing television to children's reading achievement. *Illinois School Research,* 1968, *4,* 18-21.

Lowery, L. F., and Grafft, W. Paperback books and reading attitudes. *The Reading Teacher,* 1968, *21,* 618-23.

McCracken, R. A. Do we want real readers? Guest editorial. *Journal of Reading,* 1969, *12,* 446-48.

McLaughlin, G. H. SMOG grading—a new readability formula. *Journal of Reading,* 1969, *12,* 639-46.

Nelms, B. F. Reading for pleasure in junior high school. *English Journal,* 1966, *55,* 676-81.

Petitt, Dorothy. The junior novel in the classroom. *English Journal,* 1963, *52,* 512-20.

Sakamoto, I., Hayashi, K., and Kamei, M. A developmental study on the points of inspiration in reading. *The Science of Reading,* 1967, *10,* 1-9.

Shirley, F. L. The influence of reading on adolescents. *Wilson Library Bulletin,* 1968, *43,* 256-60.

Shnayer, S. W. Some relationships between reading interests and reading comprehension. *University Microfilms (Ann Arbor) Dissertation Abstracts,* 1967, *28,* 2606. (Abstract)

Smith, R. J. The effect of reading for a creative purpose on student attitudes toward a short story. *Research in the Teaching of English,* 1968, *2* (2), 142-51.

Squire, J. R. The responses of adolescents while reading four short stories. *National Council of Teachers of English Research Report No. 2.* Champaign, Ill.: National Council of Teachers of English, 1964.

Squire, J. R., and Applebee, R. K. *High school English instruction today.* New York: Appleton-Century-Crofts, 1968.

Whitman, R. Significant reading experiences of superior English students. *Illinois English Bulletin,* 1964, *51* (5), 1-24.

Whitworth, R. G. An appraisal of the problems experienced by and the techniques used by English teachers in Indianapolis, Indiana, secondary schools in improving students' reading tastes. *University Microfilms (Ann Arbor) Dissertation Abstracts,* 1964, *25,* 5661. (Abstract)

Wilson, J. R. Responses of college freshmen to three novels. *National*

Council of Teachers of English Research Report No. 7. Champaign, Ill.: National Council of Teachers of English, 1966.

Witty, P. Studies of mass media—1949-1965. *Science Education,* 1966, *50,* 119-26.

Worley, S. E. Developmental task situations in stories. *The Reading Teacher,* 1967, *21,* 145-48.

Additional References

Appleby, B. C. The effects of individualized reading on certain aspects of literature study with high school seniors. *University Microfilms (Ann Arbor) Dissertation Abstracts,* 1967, *28,* 2592. (Abstract)

Beaver, J. C. Transformational grammar and the teaching of reading. *Research in the Teaching of English,* 1968, *2* (2), 161-71.

Bormuth, J. R., and MacDonald, O. L. Cloze tests as a measure of ability to detect literary style. In J. A. Figurel (Ed.), Reading and inquiry. *Proceedings of the International Reading Association,* 1965, *10,* 287-90.

Brittain, Mary M., and Brittain, C. V. A study at two levels of reading, cognition, and convergent thinking. *Education,* 1968, *88,* 321-25.

Brown, C. T. Three studies of the listening of children. *Speech Monographs,* 1965, *32,* 129-38.

Brown, K. L. Speech and listening in language arts textbooks: part I; part II. *Elementary English,* 1967, *44,* 336-41; 461-65, 467.

Cody, Mother M. Irene. An investigation of the relative effectiveness of four modes of presenting meaningful material to twelfth-grade students. *University Microfilms (Ann Arbor) Dissertation Abstracts,* 1962, *23,* 1270-71. (Abstract)

Cooper, J. L. The effect of training in listening on reading achievement. In J. A. Figurel (Ed.), Vistas in reading. *Proceedings of the International Reading Association,* 1966, *11* (1), 431-34.

Crippen, D. Written lesson: four methods of presentation. *Elementary School Journal,* 1968, *68,* 195-98.

Davis, O. L., Jr., and Seifert, Joan. Some linguistic features of five literature books for children. *Elementary English,* 1967, *64,* 878-82.

DeLancey, R. W. Awareness of form class as a factor in reading comprehension. *University Microfilms (Ann Arbor) Dissertation Abstracts,* 1963, *23,* 2975. (Abstract)

Devine, T. G. Listening. *Review of Educational Research*, 1967, *37*, 152-58.

Devine, T. G. Reading and listening: new research findings. *Elementary English*, 1968, *65*, 346-48.

Fishco, D. T. A study of the relationship between creativity in writing and comprehension in reading of selected seventh grade students. *University Microfilms (Ann Arbor) Dissertation Abstracts*, 1967, *27*, 3220-21. (Abstract)

Hampleman, R. S. Comparison of listening and reading comprehension ability of fourth and sixth grade pupils. *Elementary English*, 1958, *35*, 49-53.

Hasselriis, P. Effects on reading skill and social studies achievement from three modes of presentation: simultaneous reading-listening, listening, and reading. Unpublished doctoral dissertation, Syracuse University, 1968.

Hollingsworth, P. M. Can training in listening improve reading? *The Reading Teacher*, 1964, *18*, 121-23.

Hunt, K. W. Recent measures in syntactic development. *Elementary English*, 1966, *43*, 732-39.

Jarvis, O. T. Time allotment relationships to pupil achievement. *Elementary English*, 1965, *42*, 201-04, 210.

Kaufman, M. Will instruction in reading Spanish affect ability in reading English? *Journal of Reading*, 1968, *11*, 521-27.

Kingston, A. J. (Ed.) Research for the classroom: developing critical reading abilities, by W. Eller and Judith G. Wolf. *Journal of Reading*, 1966, *10*, 192-98.

Kingston, A. J. (Ed.) Research for the classroom: linguistic research and the teaching of reading, by T. G. Devine. *Journal of Reading*, 1966, *9*, 273-77.

Kingston, A. J. (Ed.) Research for the classroom: using context to determine meanings in high school and college, by L. E. Hafner. *Journal of Reading*, 1967, *10*, 491-98.

Kraner, R. E. A comparison of two methods of listening and reading training in an eighth grade language arts program. *University Microfilms (Ann Arbor) Dissertation Abstracts*, 1963, *25*, 1046. (Abstract)

Lamana, P. A. A summary of research on spelling as related to other areas of the language arts. *Journal of the Reading Specialist*, 1966, *6*, 32-39.

Littrell, J. H. English teachers' attitudes toward preparation in reading.

In O. M. Haugh (Ed.) *Teaching the teacher of English.* Champaign, Ill.: National Council of Teachers of English, 1968.

Livingston, H. F. The effects of instruction in general semantics on the critical reading ability of tenth grade students. *University Microfilms (Ann Arbor) Dissertation Abstracts,* 1964, *26,* 3783-84. (Abstract)

Loban, W. D. The language of elementary school children. *National Council of Teachers of English Research Report No. 1.* Champaign, Ill.: National Council of Teachers of English, 1963.

Lundsteen, Sara W. Listening, reading and qualitative levels of thinking in problem solving. *California Journal of Educational Research,* 1967, *18,* 230-37.

Many, W. A. Is there really any difference? Reading vs. listening? *The Reading Teacher,* 1965, *14,* 110-13.

Marquardt, W. F. Language interference in reading. *The Reading Teacher,* 1964, *18,* 214-18.

Martin, W. I. A comparative study of listening comprehension and reading comprehension in the teaching of literature to seventh-grade pupils. Unpublished doctoral dissertation, Northwestern University, 1961.

Merson, Edna M. The influence of definite listening lessons on the improvement of listening and reading comprehension and reading vocabulary. *University Microfilms (Ann Arbor) Dissertation Abstracts,* 1961, *22,* 3120-21. (Abstract)

Morton, L. The influence of instruction in critical thinking on achievement in certain aspects of the English language arts. *University Microfilms (Ann Arbor) Dissertation Abstracts,* 1964, *26,* 2080-81. (Abstract)

O'Donnell, R. C. A study of the correlations between awareness of structural relationships in English and ability in reading comprehension. *The Journal of Experimental Education,* 1963, *31,* 313-16.

Peters, Margaret L. The influence of reading methods on spelling. *The British Journal of Educational Psychology,* 1967, *37,* 47-53.

Petty, W. T., Herold, C. P., and Stoll, Earline. *The state of knowledge about the teaching of vocabulary.* Champaign, Ill.: National Council of Teachers of English, 1968.

Plattor, Emma R., and Woestehoff, E. S. The relationship between reading manuscript and cursive writing. *Elementary English,* 1967, *44,* 50-52.

Plessas, G. P., and Ladley, Dorothea M. Spelling ability and poor reading. *Elementary School Journal,* 1963, *63,* 404-08.

Plessas, G. P., and Ladley, Dorothea M. Some implications of spelling and reading research. *Elementary English*, 1965, *42*, 142-45, 200.

Prentice, Joan L. Semantics and syntax in word learning. *Journal of Verbal Learning and Verbal Behavior*, 1966, *5* (3), 279-84.

Purves, A. C. Elements of writing about a literary work: a study of response to literature. *National Council of Teachers of English Research Report No. 9*. Champaign, Ill.: National Council of Teachers of English, 1968.

Reddin, E. Listening instruction, reading, and critical thinking. *The Reading Teacher*, 1968, *21*, 654-58.

Rogers, Charlotte D. Individual differences in interpretive responses to reading the short story at the eleventh grade level. *University Microfilms (Ann Arbor) Dissertation Abstracts*, 1965, *25*, 6318-19. (Abstract)

Row, Barbara H. Reading interests of elementary school pupils in selected schools in Muscogee County, Georgia. *University Microfilms (Ann Arbor) Dissertation Abstracts*, 1968, *28*, 4391. (Abstract)

Ruddell, R. B. Oral language and the development of other language skills. *Elementary English*, 1966, *43*, 489-98.

Shirley, F. L. Case studies of the influence of reading on adolescents. *Research in the Teaching of English*, 1969, *3* (1), 30-41.

Strang, Ruth, and Rogers, Charlotte. How do students read a short story? *English Journal*, 1965, *54*, 819-23, 829.

Strickland, Ruth. The language of elementary school children: its relationship to the language of reading textbooks and to the quality of reading of selected children. *Bulletin of the School of Education, Indiana University*, 1962, *7* (4).

Thatcher, D. A. Reading instruction, creativity, and problem-solving. *The Reading Teacher*, 1967, *21*, 235-40, 260.

Webster, Elizabeth A. A single semester experiment in teaching reading skills in a sophomore literature class. In O. M. Haugh and Edwyna F. Condon (Eds.) Studies of the language arts in grades 7-13 at the University of Kansas. *Kansas Studies in Education*, 1966, *16* (1), 39-40. (Abstract)

Weintraub, S. Research: the cloze procedure. *The Reading Teacher*, 1968, *21*, 567-71, 607.

Weintraub, S. Research: oral language and reading. *The Reading Teacher*, 1968, *21*, 769-73.

Peter Hasselriis

Reading in literature:
Student involvement is just the beginning

If the reading of literature were as instinctive for human beings as learning to fly appears to be for birds, teaching humans to read literature would parallel "teaching" fledglings to fly. But the comparison is not valid, and unless teachers bring students and literature together very carefully, they will find themselves in the unenviable position of Daedalus to Icarus, watching students plummet away from the reading of literature because they have not been equipped with the necessary skills. Squire and Applebee (1968) observed the teaching of literature in high schools with exemplary literature programs and found that

> At its best, the teaching of literature . . . help(s) readers bring to bear on a literary text all of their critical awareness and discernment, their powers of perception, their values, their emotional and intellectual commitments. It involves teaching the students how to read literature as much as teaching about an individual text. Here indeed may be one of the difficulties in schools today: too many teachers seem to think that the ultimate end of instruction in literature is knowledge of and about *Macbeth* or *Silas Marner,* rather than refinement of the processes of learning to read *Macbeth* or *Silas Marner* with insight and discrimination. (Squire and Applebee, 1968, p. 107)

This paper is an attempt to acquaint literature teachers in self-contained or specialized classrooms in grades 4 through 12 with research-based knowledge or informed opinion on how these "processes of learning to read . . ." can be included in their curricula. An extensive but necessarily limited survey of the research has been made in an attempt to discover what is known about teaching the reading of literature and what applications literature teachers can make from it. It is time to begin bridging the gap between what is discovered through research and what is done in classrooms.

The practices espoused here should build upon rather than supplant the teaching of literature as experience, exploration, or examination of life. There is no substitute in nonprint media for the breadth of experience offered by literature nor for the quality of experience and understanding of oneself or others that it affords the thoughtful reader. Teachers who agree should stand their ground, provide students with access to as wide a range of literature as possible, give them quiet places and plenty of time to read, and create opportunities to share their literary experiences. But, they should also provide their students with lessons in how to read literature more effectively.

If they do not provide such lessons, if their discussions of assignments tend to be rather unstructured and short range, then they appear to be working on the assumption that skills are developed through practice rather than through teaching. To a certain extent it is probably true that practice breeds proficiency, but if this idea is carried to an extreme, it becomes comparable to tossing a child into water to teach him to swim. Moreover the results may be the same, i.e., fear of the medium and distrust of the person who forced him into it rather than a self-confident desire to return to it in the future.

No other teacher is confronted with as wide a range of differences in the types of reading he must require of his students as is the literature teacher. When the reading of poetry, drama, short story, novel, biography, autobiography, and essay is examined and compared with the range of reading required in a typical social studies, mathematics, or science course, the differences become apparent. Within each of the genres, moreover, there is an equally wide range. For example, poetry includes types as different from one another as haiku and epic and poets as dissimilar as Ogden Nash and John Milton; novelists as various as Ray Bradbury, Howard Pease, Albert Camus, and George Eliot appear; short stories as varied as those of Ernest Hemingway, Guy de Maupassant, O. Henry, and Franz Kafka compose a unit; and drama ranges at least as widely as from the comedies of Plautus, through Shakespeare, to the theater of the absurd. The reader can choose his own examples, but the point seems clear, nonetheless. A person who is a skilled reader of Longfellow cannot automatically be viewed as a skilled reader of all poetry, nor can he be automatically viewed as being skilled in reading genres other than poetry. Moreover, the themes and settings of works that can be considered legitimate parts of literature study range from *Beowulf* to the contemporary *Autobiography of Malcolm X*. Despite all of these considerations, the fact remains that the reading of literature is the bringing together of an author's mind with that of a reader, and just as no two authors are alike, there are as many differences among readers as there are readers.

The evident need, then, is for a volume that catalogs genre by genre, author by author, theme by theme, setting by setting, and reader-type by reader-type each possible reading skill in ascending order of complexity. Obviously this would be an impossible task; obviously it would produce redundancy. There are, after all, similarities among various of the genres, among individual works within genres, and among others of the differences that have been mentioned. Research findings have indicated that problems related to areas such as vocabulary, literary form, interpretation, critical reading, flexibility, and literary appreciation occur in varying degrees across all genres. It is the purpose of this paper, therefore, to describe only the most important problems peculiar to specific genres and to emphasize the problems general to all, offering possible solutions in each case.

Problems specific to various genres
Problems related to the reading of poetry

Through the years, teachers and students alike have been

concerned with the problems involved in the reading of poetry, and researchers have tended to reflect this interest. Some of their research findings have identified problems related directly to the literary form, i.e., the way a poem appears in print and the language used, as well as to the preconceived attitudes of students toward poetry. For example, Richards (1929) was surprised to find that Cambridge undergraduate students, who by all criteria should have been skilled readers of poetry, lacked the ability to write acceptable interpretations of poems that ranged widely in literary quality and whose authors they did not know. As a result of his close analyses of the ways in which he felt students went wrong, Richards found that they were unable to handle poems as series of English sentences; therefore, they did not understand the plain sense meanings of the poems. He also found that students needed help in learning how to appreciate poetry at the sensory level and how to visualize images. They would doubtless benefit from guided practice in visualizing images such as that recommended by Sam Smiley, drama professor at the University of Missouri—Columbia. Students are directed to close their eyes and imagine persons, places, and memories that are described as they do so. Students' thoughts can be directed to their homes, to loved ones, and to events that have occurred in their pasts. This technique can easily be modified to provide a valuable adjunct to the teaching of poetry, because it tends to make students more sensitive to imagery and other devices used to evoke sensory impressions. When students are encouraged to imagine persons, places, and events similar to those in poems scheduled to be discussed, they become more aware of the multiplicity of elements that are involved both in the reading and the writing of poetry.

Finally, Richards found that generally students were unable to ignore their own preconceptions of how certain themes and poetic devices should be used. That is, they could not separate their impartial interpretations of poems from experiences and thoughts that were not related to the poems under study. This is not difficult to understand. If a person has had a strong emotional experience that is evoked by words or themes handled in

a poem, it will be very difficult for him to set his personal reactions aside and objectively entertain those of the poet. It is
conceivable, for example, for a poet to speak lovingly of ani-
mals, reptiles, persons, or events that readers would normally
find abhorrent. But if a poem is to be read with the understanding it deserves, such unrelated associations must be set
aside. Perhaps a teacher can deal with this problem by presenting a poem addressed to a given theme, having students list
every thought they had on the theme before they read the poem,
and then carefully comparing their preconceptions as objectively
as possible with the thoughts presented in the poem.

Teachers, according to Richards, must be alert to the fact
that students tend to develop "stock responses" to poems, that
they tend to view and respond to all poems on a given theme
with responses that are based not on the particular poem under
study, but rather, on the basis of similar poems that have been
studied previously.

Poetry study often elicits sentimental reactions from readers,
which is not necessarily to be deplored unless sentimentality is
a reaction that is not warranted by the poem itself. It is the responsibility of the teacher to analyze the contents of the poem
and to place appropriate, carefully justified restrictions on students' sentimental reactions. Some teachers have had success
with the use of slides and transparencies that carry such provocative titles as "I haven't had a bath in two weeks," which
the students read and discuss before they are shown a picture of
a war-weary soldier in a foxhole. Teachers can create other
examples that become more and more subtle, until they approach the level of sophistication which poetry demands and of
which their students are capable.

Research on the reading and interpretation of poetry that
examines less global problems than those addressed by Richards
is relatively sparse. Most of the studies are directed toward
problems related to specific works; therefore, application of
their findings to all poetry is limited. An example of such a
study is one by Livingston (1969) who discovered that a course
in general semantics had neither a deleterious nor a salutary ef-

fect on pupils' abilities to discover the underlying metaphor of Frost's "It Bids Pretty Fair." This is interesting though not too surprising, since it is known (Smith, 1967) that readers can be flexible and can change their reading styles according to the comprehension demands of whatever it is they are reading, but before the findings can be accepted as generally true of poetry, other studies on the relationship between instruction in semantics and metaphor interpretation must be conducted. Research has not been directed toward discovering the existence of such specific problems nor toward discovering ways to teach objective and flexible poetry reading/interpretation. Research has shown, however, that many existing textbook materials and teaching techniques are not achieving these desired results. As early as 1921, Hosic raised pertinent questions about the worth of textbook questions and exercises relative to the existing theories of poetry instruction and classroom practices; in 1968 writers such as Martin were still raising the same question, so it seems as if teachers rather than textbooks are likely to solve the problems of poetry readers.

Helping students become better readers of poetry

Given this situation, teachers must examine their present teaching methods in terms of their students' abilities and interests. Research has shown that in guiding students' interpretations of a poem it is best to start by having them examine their reactions to the work as a complete literary experience rather than by subjecting them to a detailed analysis of the elements of thought and language of which it is comprised (Hosic, 1921). Purves (1968) referred to recent findings of developmental psychologists to underscore the contention supported by Hosic's study that in the study of a poem, readers should be led from general impressions to particular aspects of it. He extended this by analogy to the reading of fiction and drama and supported the view that students should not be expected to read with the sophistication of literary critics, nor even with that of their teachers.

Yet in classes described by Gallo (1968) teachers were still observed in the process of starting their exegeses of poems with questions such as "How many alliterations did you count, Sam?" "Why isn't this a good example of a sonnet?" "Why isn't this poem as good as the one we just finished?" Total disregard of students' personal reactions was the rule rather than the exception, and the order in which poetic elements was studied was the reverse of what researchers have been recommending since the early decades of the century.

Another classroom practice brought into question by research findings is the use of biographical information about a poet whose work is being studied. Andrews (1970) found that including the biography of a poem's author along with a taped presentation of the poem did not affect either the comprehension of the poem nor the extent to which students liked it. In many literature anthologies, however, it is possible to find entire pages given over to pictures and information about poets whose works are represented on far less space. The implication here seems to be that only biography relevant to a poem is important. Biography for biography's sake contributes little to a student's understanding and appreciation of a particular work.

Weekes' (1929) research concerned the problem of content selection. Her findings indicated that teachers should choose poems for classroom reading that are based on topics with which their students are familiar. This does not mean that classroom selections should never go beyond the experiential background of students; if such were the case, the students would learn little from their poetry reading. However, it does indicate that if teachers in places like Kansas are determined to teach poems like "Sea Fever," and if they want their students to comprehend and like these poems, they had best be sure that their students are relatively familiar with and interested in sea life.

Also, works studied as parts of our literary heritage are deserving of much more advance preparation than, "This is great, and I am sure you will like it for that reason." Presentations of *Beowulf* need not become extended discussions of Norse sagas with similar legends, multiple or single authorship, and life in sixth-century northern Europe, but, in order to bring the students of this decade to an appreciation of the universality of the epic's themes, it may first be necessary to bring them to the point that they are receptive to learning anything at all about it. It seems fair to say that anything pertinent to an understanding of poetic works that are not immediately comprehensible to students should be presented to them before they are asked to read, understand, or appreciate the works.

Finally, Weekes (1929) found a strong correlation between a student's appreciation of a poem and his comprehension of it. She also found that students had greater relative difficulty with the comprehension of figurative language than with involved sentence structure in poetry. The obvious implication here is that classroom assistance in the comprehension of figurative language must be provided.

There are undoubtedly as many ways of teaching figurative language as there are different types of figurative language, so there are no simple suggestions to guide teachers in this task. Emphasis, however, should be on the accurate interpretation and understanding of such language rather than on the technical terms used by scholars to describe it. It is far more important for a reader to know that when a poet uses the word *sail* he is referring to an entire ship—if indeed that is his intent—than it is for him to be able to define the word *synecdoche*. It is more important for a reader to be able to understand and appreciate Robert Frost's use of the word *play* in the poem "It Bids Pretty Fair" than it is for him to write the word *metaphor* on an answer sheet.[1]

It also seems fair to say that if a literary work has no effect

---

[1]"It Bids Pretty Fair"

> The play seems out for an almost infinite run.
> Don't mind a little thing like the actors fighting.
> The only thing I worry about is the sun.
> We'll be all right if nothing goes wrong with the lighting.

From *The Poetry of Robert Frost*, edited by Edward Connery Lathem, p. 392. Copyright 1947 by Holt, Rinehart and Winston, Inc. Reprinted by permission of Holt, Rinehart and Winston, Inc.

on a reader, even after he has been carefully prep...
it, further study of the work should be discontinued. The ...
mon practice of establishing an entire year's course of study before any students have entered the building is unreasonable if teachers accept the fact that student interest and involvement are at least as important to consider as the content and reading difficulty of the materials used. Students should be given the opportunity to help choose the selections they are taught, and teachers should be flexible enough to allow students to stop reading and studying selections with which they discover unanticipated difficulties or antipathies. There is certainly enough literature of all types available that it need be an extremely rare occasion to ask a student to read and study something he does not like. This does not imply that teachers should abrogate their responsibility to motivate students to read unfamiliar materials, but it does ask teachers to relax the requirement that all students read identical selections and to entertain the idea that from time to time a student may decide not to complete a selection.

Problems related to the reading of short stories

The reading of short stories offers unique challenges to readers and, like poetry, provides teachers with entire works of art that can be examined in relatively short periods of time. Aside from the obvious difficulties posed by unfamiliar vocabulary and concepts, there are considerations similar to those discovered by Richards with readers of poetry that also apply to readers of short stories.

Squire (1964) found that American teenagers reading short stories erred in their oral responses to them in ways that were similar to the errors in Richards' students' written reactions to poetry. Again some problems were the result of characteristics of the particular literary form and others the result of preconceived student ideas. Students failed to grasp the essential meaning of narratives. They failed to understand key words, did not understand the implications of details, and tended to make incorrect inferences. They did not suspend judgment and thereby did not change initial judgments in relation to details presented later in the stories. As in Richards' investigation, students tended to rely on stock responses. Squire found that American teenagers consistently reacted to stories according to their preconceptions of the following five themes:

1] Adolescents are not responsible for their own actions.
2] A boy or girl in trouble doesn't have a very healthy home life.
3] Wealth and happiness are incompatible.
4] When adults and adolescents are in conflict, the adults are almost always wrong.
5] Punishment for adolescent wrongdoing accomplishes little or should be avoided. (1964, p. 40)

Squire concluded that it does not matter whether one agrees to look at situations realistically. They demanded happy end-substitutes for independent thinking. Readers should not use clichés as substitutes for thinking, and they should learn to recognize when writers use them to capitalize on readers' stock responses.

Another failing evidenced by students in Squire's investigation was happiness binding, or a refusal on the part of students to look at situations realistically. They demanded happy endings and attributed incorrect motives to the actions of characters. They brought to their reading critical predispositions as to what constitutes a good or a poor short story, using set criteria whether or not they were applicable to the stories in question, tending to demand "typical" or "true life" situations and "good description." They made irrelevant associations and tended to associate events in stories with personal experiences, memories of fiction, motion pictures, radio, and television. They were also diverted from an accurate interpretation of a particular story when it reminded them of other stories they had read. Finally, they tended to fill in aspects of character or plot that might have been intentionally left out by an author.

Helping students become better readers of short stories

A variety of remedies for helping students become more skilled short story readers suggest themselves. One is to ask students to read and react to what they have read, with the teacher correcting their reactions accordingly. But this method contains elements of correction given after the fact that would probably have adverse effects on the motivation of all except the students who read with relatively few errors. Teachers should instead take time to discuss the pitfalls that researchers such as Richards (1929) and Squire (1964) have indicated students are likely to encounter and to teach ways of avoiding them such as the ones previously suggested.

Students should be given the opportunity to read as wide a variety of poetry and short stories as possible, and classes should be structured in such ways as to allow readers to respond freely to what they have read. Subdividing classes into small discussion groups is an extremely effective way of providing students with the opportunity to discuss their reading with no fear of appearing naive or foolish to the teacher. But too often such discussion groups wander from their assigned topics. Reading and reasoning guides such as those advocated in Vine, et al. (1967) and in Herber (1970) can be used to structure the responses of individuals along the lines implied by the problems uncovered by Richards and Squire, and they can also be designed to provide a structured but unrestrictive framework for group discussions. For example, if a teacher is interested in teaching students the relative effectiveness of various endings to a short story (attempting to circumvent the "happiness binding" described by Squire), he might provide students with a guide that contains examples of story endings which differ from the one provided by the author. The teacher's reading guide might contain questions designed to draw from the students the conclusion that the contrived endings do not logically follow the preceding story elements, are unrealistic, or cannot be justified for other reasons. After reading the variant and real endings and reacting to the task of the guide on an individual basis, stu-

41

compare their reactions to those of other students
up discussions and resolve any differences they
might find. The role of the teacher in such cases is to provide
the initial guidance and to participate in the group discussions
when it becomes evident that his help is needed. If he wishes,
he can lead a whole class discussion to summarize the understandings that have evolved as a result of the individual and
group work.

Examples of guides similar to the one described and exercises designed to help students arrive at conclusions concerning
a wide variety of literature reading skills are contained in the
sources alluded to previously as well as in certain literature anthology workbooks. (See Vine, Vine, and Jewitt, 1968, and
Vine, et al., 1968.)

Problems related to the reading of other genres

The investigations of Richards (1929) and Squire (1964)
have provided at least starting points from which teachers can
improve their students' understandings of poetry and short stories, but researchers have not as yet provided similar information specifically designed for the reading of other genres. How
a student can most effectively read novels, dramatic literature,
essays, biographies, autobiographies, and other literary types
has not yet precisely been determined. This is not to say that a
teacher can justify not teaching specific ways of reading such
forms, since his own extensive personal experience does now
and will always provide him with a great deal of information
that future research will likely support. His experience as a
reader as well as the research information provided from studies
of such genres as poems and short stories will be more than
adequate for helping him list the problems that are likely to be
encountered by his students as they read the works he assigns.

Novels. Novels, after all, can often be viewed as long short
stories, so there is certainly carryover from the study of short
stories to the study of novels. (For example, Wilson, 1966,
used the response categories outlined by Squire, 1964, for

short stories to categorize the reactions of college students to novels.) The same critical reading skills which enable students to understand and correctly interpret key words, detail, character development, and theme in short stories should be emphasized with novels. Also, the subjective responses which produce "happiness binding" should be given special attention.

Drama. Since there is less carryover with other genres, it becomes the teacher's responsibility to determine what is needed by his students. When teaching drama, he will undoubtedly emphasize such skills as close reading of stage directions and descriptions of settings and characters; he will probably try to show his students the importance of visualizing stage sets, lighting, costumes, and the movement of characters; and he will probably deem it important to direct his students to an inward "listening" to the voices of the players. Above and beyond considerations such as these, he will probably be concerned that his students account for the gaps in meaning that are unique to drama, that is, events which have taken place at a time prior to that being described must be inferred by readers from the speeches of the actors.

The teacher may also want to structure his approach to drama so that it results in a developmental sequence. For example, he could begin by having his students read one-act plays. Since reading time is usually comparable to acting time—rarely over an hour—the one-act play fits nicely into the time limits of a class period. Moreover, it seems reasonable that the beginning reader of dramatic literature should be fairly well grounded in the reading of these shorter forms of the art before he is asked —or expected—to tackle the longer forms. The one-act plays could be followed by full-length, uncomplicated modern plays, and the sequence could be culminated with the reading of Shakespearean plays and difficult contemporary works. It is now rather common for Shakespeare to be the first playwright with whom students are brought in contact, a circumstance that does not seem reasonable.

Although this admittedly sketchy discussion has emphasized

the study of drama as the study of plays read silently by students rather than the study of plays performed live or on film, it does not mean to imply that the study of drama as a performing art should be ignored in curricula. Rather, it indicates that to this author the two are not the same. When a play is read silently, the reader can pore over dialogue, digest the playwright's directions to the players, and perform a variety of other activities that are not possible for members of a live audience. Moreover, there are aspects of watching plays that are so different from the phenomena that are available to the reader of a play that they must be taught in their own right. It is difficult, if not impossible, to achieve the total effect of costumes, stage movement, lights, sound effects, sets, and the voices of actors, coupled with the subliminal interaction among actors and audience that is akin to the charismatic effect of a dynamic public speaker, a sunset, or beautiful music, from the printed page alone without much practice and training. It thereby behooves teachers who want their pupils to become skilled readers as well as appreciative but critical viewers of plays to provide them with teaching in both. Too often, students get the impression that plays are a written form rather than a performed one. Instead of using the forms as complements of each other, teachers imply that they are separate.

Expository writing. As people progress through school and through life beyond school, they will be confronted with the need to read increasingly abundant and increasingly difficult expository writing. The formal essay is one small example of this type, and its study legitimately forms a part of the study of our literary heritage. However, as far as mandatory reading is concerned, the formal essay probably will constitute but a small part.

Any person who takes a position with virtually any arm of government, for example, will rapidly be asked to read and assimilate mountains of reports that are written in styles of English that students do not yet know exist. Members of large corporations will be required to read reports of all types, as will persons involved in almost every line of work that can be imagined, ranging from agriculture, to engineering, to school teaching, to law, to medicine. Moreover, every repairman, salesman, and building custodian will have times when he must read in order to keep up with the new developments in his work. And the material provided in newspapers and magazines that must be read for information on topics related to life outside of a person's occupation composes no small proportion of his total reading of expository writing.

This paper is not the place to consider specifically what types of expository writing should become integrated among the literary forms that are more commonly taught, and there is a question whether instruction in reading such writing is the sole responsibility of the literature teacher, but if students are not given systematic instruction in how to improve their reading of such vitally important types of writing, then there is no doubt that the language arts teacher should incorporate it into his curriculum. Such training should, moreover, include aspects of critical reading study, and instruction in it should begin as soon as students are capable of learning from the printed page.

Helping students become better readers of other genres

In regard to the improvement of the reading of novels, Wilson (1966) found that class study, including teacher-led and panel discussions, caused changes in the types of responses students made toward the novels they read. Alluding again to the types of responses isolated by Squire (1964), i.e., literary judgment, interpretational, narrational, associational, self-involvement, prescriptive, and miscellaneous, the major type of change was toward those categorized as interpretational. In Wilson's words

> . . . Student responses changed after study to increased efforts at interpretation at the expense of nearly all other categories of response, including literary judgment.
>
> Individual analysis showed that responses coded interpretational were usually more analytic and objective than

the facile labeling which sometimes constituted literary judgment. Thus the increase in interpretation over literary judgment would indicate more maturity of perception, a desirable result of the study of literature. (Wilson, 1966, p. 43)

It is difficult to make specific recommendations for the improvement of instruction in the reading of plays and essays. However, there is an implication in almost all that has been said so far that the reading of literature involves skills that a teacher should teach, skills that apply in various ways across the genres. This viewpoint appears to run counter to that of persons who advocate that literature should primarily be experienced by readers and that a student's experiencing of literature should not be stifled or restricted by a teacher. If there were no other choice available, one would agree with the efficacy of unrestricted literary experience. Nothing is more harmful to the developing of appreciation or proficiency in the reading of literature than overdoing the job of discussing, analyzing, criticizing, or, at the worst, imposing the interpretation of a skilled reader upon that of a neophyte. But teachers have a choice and should, therefore, make every attempt to satisfy both objectives, i.e., they should seek ways to provide students with unrestricted literary experiences and provide them with guidance that will heighten the effectiveness of their future literary experiences.

There is no longer a place for the teacher who is so afraid of stifling a student's interest in poetry, for example, that he smiles and nods at every asinine, unsupported interpretation his pupils voice. A music teacher knows music well enough to tell when wrong notes or rhythms are being played. He also knows stages in the development of young musicians well enough to know how strict to be in his demands for pieces being played up to tempo, for perfect intonation, or for adequate tone quality, and he is careful not to set his objectives so high as to frustrate rather than challenge his pupils. Just so, a teacher of literature must impose limits of reason on the interpretations of students and at the same time allow for their lack of skill and experience. It is not realistic to think that saturation and unguided practice

can be considered substitutes for teaching, and it is eq̲ ̲ ̲
realistic to think that there are not myriads of frustrated readers
in today's classrooms.

Problems applicable to all genres

Vocabulary: general

As a teacher becomes concerned with helping students improve general reading skills as well as the skills specific to reading different literary genres, he will find vocabulary development to be a major facet of reading instruction. Davis (1968)
found recalling word meanings to be basic to reading comprehension and recommended that teachers use every possible way
of introducing students to new words. Possible methods that he
suggested ranged from books, writing assignments, field trips,
discussions, and visual aids to ". . . a graded series of passages
that introduce the most generally useful words in appropriate
contexts." (p. 543)

Petty, Herold, and Stoll (1968) pointed out that research
has not yet discovered whether it is more effective to teach the
meanings of words directly, or indirectly through context, although research by Ames (1966, 1970) and Quealy (1969) indicates that specific types of context clues isolated by researchers may lead to specific recommendations as to how such clues
should be taught. It is also not clear whether an inductive or
deductive approach to the teaching of vocabulary is better.
The final decision on methodology is therefore left, at this point,
to the judgment of the individual teacher. However, the
teacher should be reminded of the fact that much teaching of
vocabulary in grades 4 through 12 is predicated more on text
materials writers' decisions than on pupils' needs. Teachers use
the traditional vocabulary workbooks and do not thereby take
individual differences in vocabulary development into account.
Some of their students know the twenty or so words introduced
in a unit without any further instruction, while others may not
know any of them. To ask all of the students to do identical

exercises and take the same test over the meanings of the words does not make sense.

Word selection. Regardless of the criteria used to select the words in such predetermined lists, they will be related to the other activities that are taking place in the literature classroom only by chance. Some few words may appear concurrently in the reading and vocabulary assignments; a greater number will not. This study of vocabulary in relative isolation rather than as an integral part of the subject content is often questioned. For example, regarding the choice of words to be included in vocabulary study, Vine, *et al.* (1967) and Herber (1970) advocated placing the emphasis on words students encounter in their assigned readings. They recommended that teachers survey the materials they plan to ask students to read, list the important words students are not likely to know, and teach those words. They advocated presenting the words to the students before the reading is assigned so that not knowing them will not detract from the reading experience. On the other hand, they noted that a teacher must bear in mind the fact that he may present too many words and therefore render the reading anti-climactic. He will need to include some words and delete others because of the possibility that their inclusion or exclusion will lessen the impact of the literary work for its reader.

The most serious criticism of the study of preselected vocabulary in isolation is that it does not do an adequate job of teaching word meanings to students. Too often students must memorize single definitions of words and some of their common synonyms or antonyms. Students are not given an opportunity to bring forth their own experiences with the words, nor are they given time to try words out, discuss them with their peers, read them in contexts other than the short sentences in the lessons, or see them used figuratively. They are not given systematic instruction in semantics, examining such elements as connotations, denotations, or euphemisms; they do not examine words used in propagandistic contexts; and they rarely go into the sorts of things that help build interest in word study for its own sake. Vocabulary workbooks ignore interesting etymologies, unusual words like *antidisestablishmentarianism* and *pneumonoultramicroscopicsilicovolcanokoniosis,* and such phenomena as palindromes, acronyms, or Tom Swifties.

The development of word meaning skills. Besides teaching students the meanings of unfamiliar words, teachers should also help them develop independence in learning the meanings of unfamiliar words. There is a good deal more to this than telling students to use the dictionary to find the meanings of any words they do not know. Teachers should consult such research as that of Ames (1966, 1970) and Quealy (1969), previously cited, to find specific ways in which context clues can assist in word meaning skills, and they should read Deighton (1959), who shows how structural analysis, that is, knowledge of the meanings of carefully specified prefixes, suffixes, and roots, can assist readers in discovering the meanings of unfamiliar words. Whenever possible, formal lessons in context and structural analyses should be taught, and whenever such teaching can be combined with or related to other teaching, it should be.

Vocabulary reinforcement. After the meanings of important words have been taught, context clues and structural principles introduced, and the literature selection read, word study should continue with more than a weekly test in which the directions read, "Use the following words in a paragraph, showing by their use that you know what they mean." The old saw, "Use a word three times and it's yours," cannot be supported and could not be even it if were true that large numbers of words have only single meanings in all contexts. Some students can see a given word for the first time in their lives and "know" it from then on, while others need to see it many more times before this becomes true. Some words, on the other hand, carry such complex meanings that learners of all ages must continue to add to and refine their conceptions of them. It is therefore extremely important that teachers provide ways in which students can reinforce and extend their knowledge of the words that have presented. Teachers can create paper and pencil exercises for this purpose using guidelines described in the films and manuals and book alluded to previously: Vine *et al.* 1967; Herber, 1964, 1970. Some of the described reinforcement exercises are designed to elicit specific recall of definitions, a purpose that teachers may find useful from time to time, but many are designed to evoke thoughts and discussion at a much deeper level of understanding.

In short, literature teachers' sources of words and opportunities for making word study profitable and interesting are unlimited unless such teachers choose to use a packaged vocabulary text. Words can be drawn from selections a teacher plans to read aloud to his students, from literature that students are reading for class work, from words listed by students in their personal lists of unknown words, and from words garnered from such sources as radio, television, or films. Moreover, it is essential that words in a given word study program be introduced many times to ensure that students have learned them, and it is essential that the words chosen be of obvious personal relevance to the students who are expected to learn and like learning them.

Vocabulary: technical

General vocabulary development, however, is only one aspect of vocabulary instruction in the literature classroom. Teachers of literature are confronted with a technical vocabulary comprised of terms used to describe various aspects of literature study. Frank (1970) in recommending that teachers use linguistics to teach poetry used, among others, the following technical terms:

phonology	diction	primary stress
syntax	morphology	colloquial idioms
meter	philologists	prosody
iambic pentameter	metrical feet	stress patterns
indefinite plurals	scanning	metrical patterns
bisyllabic	abstract nouns	articles
prepositions	trochaic	spondees

imagery	conjunctions	quatrain
grammatical patterning	metrical variation	secondary stress
stops	pyrrhic	caesura
conventional orthography	dental stops	assonance
phoneme	tertiary stress	grapheme
syntactic inversion	onomatopoetic object	symbols
enjambed lines	metonymic	verb
		personification

(Frank, 1970, pp. 948-53)

Some of the terms are relatively common, at least to teachers of literature, but many are not. The question that each teacher must resolve for himself and for his students is whether it is necessary for students to know such terms in order to understand and appreciate poetry and other forms of literature.

Such terms are certainly not limited to poetry but are found associated with all other genres as well. Discussions of short stories, for example, are often in terms of *plots, characters, conflicts,* and *climaxes;* plays are referred to as *comedies* or *tragedies* containing *acts, scenes,* and *settings;* and the words *formal, informal,* and *expository* are among those used in descriptions of essays.

The question becomes not how these terms should be introduced but whether they should be taught at all. They are needed by persons who find it necessary or desirable to talk or write about literature, but it is questionable whether knowing them is a necessary part of experiencing or enjoying literature. Just as a film viewer can experience a film without knowing the terms *dolly, close-up,* or *dissolve,* or a listener can experience music without knowing *rallentando, sostenuto,* or *sforzando,* a reader or listener can experience a poem without knowing the words *conceit, chiasmus,* or *caesura.*

Some students will undoubtedly reach the point at which their understanding of literature will require the introduction of these terms, but, to the extent that their introduction detracts from a student's enjoyment, or experiencing of literature, it is to be deplored. Which, for example, will help heighten a student's awareness of literature and its relationship to his own life more, a discussion of why a poet decided to compare the two things he decided to compare or a statement such as, "Look, class, on line 12 there is an example of a simile."?

When a teacher does decide to introduce literature's technical vocabulary to his students, he should use the same criteria that he does in choosing words to be added to his students' general vocabularies. If such terms are used often and become integrated closely within the day-by-day reading/writing activities and discussions of a class, they will be useful to students and will be retained by them. To require memorization of such terms without closely relating them to students' experiences is asking for the typical, "I learned them for the test and forgot them the following day."

Literary interpretation: teaching aids and materials

Although students cannot understand a literary work without understanding its vocabulary, such understanding as well as literal comprehension are only the first steps in comprehending literature. Interpretation is another major factor which must be incorporated into the instructional procedure of the literature classroom.[2]

Instructional framework/directed reading lesson.
Teachers who do not provide instruction prior to assigning reading are, in Herber's (1970) terms, "assuming" rather than "assuring" that their students possess the necessary reading skills they might

---

[2] It should be noted that interpretation as it is treated here is explication, not oral reading. Authorities in reading instruction have been advocating that the teaching of reading be the teaching of silent reading since at least 1920 (Smith, 1934). It is emphasized that although some reading problems of less able readers may be identified through the relatively common practice of having students read orally around the room during their classes many poor readers do not volunteer to read aloud and capable readers rebel against listening to unrehearsed readings that they have strong reasons for feeling are not as good as theirs would be. This practice therefore tends to inhibit a student's interest in and appreciation of a literary work. Oral reading by the teacher, on the other hand, is a practice that is widely recommended for helping to increase appreciation in literature. Such writers as Joll (1963), Huus (1963), and Farrell (1966) advocate that a fairly substantial amount of time be devoted to teacher prepared oral interpretations of short stories and poems. In fact, such presentations can be very effective introductions to literary selections because of the interest they create. Once student enthusiasm is aroused, classroom instruction for explication/interpretation can begin.

very well have expected to learn in their literature course. Such "assumptive teaching," as Herber refers to it, seems to be fairly widespread, and it manifests itself in areas other than reading as well. Teachers who tell their students they want them to write compositions, for instance, and who do not tell them what criteria they will be evaluated upon until the work is returned are exemplifying assumptive teaching. Rather than discussing specific objectives that are mutually agreed upon with the students, such teachers inform students through the "errors" in their papers. Teachers who begin the study of novels with silent readings that are followed by teacher-question, class-response activities are making assumptions of their students' reading skills, also. However, such teaching methods can be avoided easily. Herber (1970) offers a model for structuring lessons, the Instructional Framework, that can be used as a basis for adding preparatory steps and reading guidance to teaching procedures, and teachers of reading use a similar structure that is commonly called the Directed Reading Lesson.

A Directed Reading Lesson is normally considered to consist of three stages: preparation, directed reading, and followup. A teacher examines the text he wants his students to read, isolates vocabulary words he thinks might be unfamiliar and determines if any of the concepts contained within the selection will be unclear to students unless they are provided with additional background information. He also determines for what purposes he thinks his students should read. Thus, the teaching of vocabulary, the preparation of concept learning, and the setting of purposes comprise the usual parts of a Directed Reading Lesson's preparation step. This step is followed by silent reading and followup. During the followup, the teacher usually leads discussions of the content, attempting to help students relate what they have read to their own lives, and he attempts to help students clear up misunderstandings that might have arisen during the reading and discussion. Typical followup activities might include small-group discussions, viewing films or filmstrips, listening to tapes or records, written assignments, and quizzes. What is considered important is that teachers be sure that students possess the skills and understandings needed to comprehend and appreciate what they have been asked to read. This implies that assigned readings should be directed: that students should be instructed in what to look for, how the reading should be approached, and what specific reading skills will be needed.

Herber's Instructional Framework maintains essentially the same outline as the Directed Reading Lesson but provides ways of adding structured guidance for both the reading itself and for students' reactions to it. Herber's model is designed for use by teachers of subject matter content classes and is therefore more applicable in these classes than is the Directed Reading Lesson. The Instructional Framework is designed as a structure through which both subject matter and reading skills are taught, whereas the Directed Reading Lesson places greater emphasis on reading skills.

The profundity scale.   Another structure that teachers might find useful is the Profundity Scale, developed by Andresen (1966), which is designed to afford students and teachers with a way to discover and evaluate the depth of an author's themes.   The rationale behind presenting students with such a model is given below:

> The reading of narrative materials . . . is primarily a personal process. Consequently, creative students who are presented interesting selections to read by a knowledgeable and dynamic teacher will invent their own approaches for reading narrative material. Yet, developing such reading techniques is often difficult for the average student. These students are often aided in reading narration if they are taught a theoretical construct to guide their thinking. The Profundity Scale is an example of such a construct. Specifically, the Profundity Scale was devised to aid the reader in determining and evaluating the profundity of an author's theme. (Sargent, Huus, and Andresen, 1970, p. 28)

The scale is on five planes: the physical, mental, moral, psychological, and philosophical. An example showing how it might be related to Mitchell's *Gone With the Wind* is given below:

> *Physical Plane:* Reader is aware primarily only of the physical actions of the characters. Example: The battle scenes and the burning of Atlanta.
>
> *Mental Plane:* Reader is aware of the physical and intellectual actions of the characters. Example: The machinations of Scarlet O'Hara.
>
> *Moral Plane:* Reader is aware of the physical and intellectual actions of characters in light of an ethical code. Example: Scarlet's endeavor to win the affections of Ashley Wilkes.
>
> *Psychological Plane:* Reader is aware of the psychological forces influencing the characters' physical and intellectual actions in light of an ethical code. Example: Scarlet's rebellion against the social mores of the Old South.
>
> *Philosophical Plane:* Reader is aware of the universal truths expounded by the author through the physical, intellectual, and ethical behavior of the characters under the influence of psychological forces. Example: The pageant of the decline of the way of life of the Old South. (Sargent, Huus, and Andresen, 1970, p. 29)

Two possible methods of employing the Profundity Scale are advocated. First, when a student reads narration, he determines what is happening at each of the five levels, and, second, he evaluates or judges ". . . the effectiveness of the selection at each level." (Sargent, Huus, and Andresen, 1970, p. 30)

There are some who will argue against such a model as being too restrictive of students' responses, and for bright students who are capable of organizing their responses to literature independently of such imposed models as the Profundity Scale, the critics have a valid point. But it can be counter-argued that there are many students who need such a device as this upon which to base at least their initial judgments of narrational material. It appears quite superior to judging works by the emimence of their authors or by meek acceptance of the opinions of peers or teachers.

Programed instruction. An approach to helping students interpret literature that would appear to be much more restrictive of their personal reactions was described in detail by Reid (1963) in an article in which he explained the stages in writing programed lessons for the intensive study of literature. A portion of a program written for the study of Frost's "Stopping by Woods on a Snowy Evening" was provided so that teachers might experience programed instruction for themselves before judging its effectiveness. Reid stated that his objectives for writing programed lessons were

1] to improve the attitude of high school students toward poetry:

2] to start students developing for themselves a method which can become a permanent part of their repertoire for reading poems in depth. (Reid, 1963, p. 658)

He also discussed the use of programed instruction for teaching general reading improvement skills, the reading of short stories, novels, and recognized literary classics. He provided the titles and sources of a large number of programs that have already been written and field tested. The reactions of most students and teachers who used the programed texts appeared to be quite favorable, and the method is therefore one that bears close scrutiny by teachers of the reading of literature.

Use of authors' rough drafts. Another interpretation technique which often creates student interest by providing insight into the ideas behind and the evolution of a particular work is the use of rough drafts. Such a technique is especially effective with poetry, but it is certainly not limited to the genre.

Over three pages of the *English Journal* feature, "Poetry in the Classroom," (now discontinued) were devoted to a discussion of Robert Frost's "Nothing Gold Can Stay." (Quinn, 1966) It is an extended interpretation of the poem which includes insight into Frost's philosophy as it is revealed in the poem. Any teacher with questions as to the poetic devices used or the meaning of the poem is certainly advised to consult this source. But this article, like many others that have been written, are now being written, and will continue to be written, may not be as helpful to the teacher as it appears. Such articles deal with poetry at a level commensurate with the understandings, backgrounds, and skills of teachers or prospective teachers, and their prescriptions cannot be directly implemented with elementary, junior, or senior high school students. The teacher must be very careful to help his students make the transition from where they are to a point nearer the levels attained by the journal authors, literary critics, and other skilled persons to whom the articles are directed.

One method that teachers might find useful in helping students to discover for themselves some of the insights provided in such articles is the use of authors' rough drafts of the works discussed. They might find it interesting and profitable, for example, to discuss reasons for a poet's choosing certain words in preference to others, or they might read all available drafts without knowing which was finally deemed publishable and be required to support their decisions as to which is the most effective. A quick reading of two drafts of "Nothing Gold Can Stay" will illustrate the possibilities of this teaching technique:

"Nothing Gold Can Stay" by Robert Frost

Early Draft:[3]

> Nature's first green is gold
> Her hardest hue to hold.
> Her early leaves are flowers;
> But only so for hours.
> Then leaves subside to leaves.
> In autumn she achieves
> A still more golden blaze.
> But nothing golden stays.

---

[3]The early draft was submitted by Miss Nancy Wolpers as part of a class assignment made by the author at the University of Missouri-Columbia, Spring, 1970. The original source is not known. The final draft is from *The Poetry of Robert Frost*, edited by Edward Connery Lathem, p. 222. Copyright 1923 by Holt, Rinehart and Winston, Inc. Copyright 1951 by Robert Frost. Reprinted by permission of Holt, Rinehart and Winston, Inc.

Final Draft:

> Nature's first green is gold,
> Her hardest hue to hold.
> Her early leaf's a flower;
> But only so an hour.
> Then leaf subsides to leaf.
> So Eden sank to grief,
> So dawn goes down to day.
> Nothing gold can stay.

Richard Wilbur has used drafts of his poems during presentations to teachers to illustrate revisions that were made before a poem's final form, and the author has seen parts of six versions of Yeat's "Leda and the Swan." Such drafts are fascinating to students of literature and are, therefore, a valuable addition to a teacher's repertory.

Comparing works of dissimilar quality. A similar technique but one that also helps students refine their ways of deciding whether selections are good or poor examples of literature is for a teacher to provide copies of pairs of poems with the poets' names omitted so that class discussions of poetic devices, settings, style, and worth cannot be influenced by the names. Two poems on a similar theme but of differing quality can be used to help give students practice in comprehending poetry as well as in developing literary taste. Sparke and McKowen (1970) used this technique in their college freshman composition text *Montage: Investigations in Language.* One of their examples is a page on which Phillip Booth's "Vermont: Indian Summer" and Edgar Guest's "The Call" are printed without any identification except for titles. Students, who it is presumed are not familiar with either poem, are asked to choose the poem they judge to be superior and to defend their choice.

Rottenberg (1963) turned the question, "How do you know a book is good unless you read some bad ones?" to her advantage. She used Henry James's criteria for evaluating novels written in the realistic tradition as a model for discussing two contemporary books chosen particularly because they did not come up to James's standards. Two novels by Taylor Caldwell, *The Final Hour* and *Your Sins and Mine,* were used in Rottenberg's lessons.

It is a mistake for teachers not to use exercises such as those that have been described. It is too easy to give pupils the impression that everything in print is excellent merely because it is in print. (Literature anthologies should probably assume a large share of the responsibility for the promotion of this delusion.) It is a teacher's responsibility to see that students learn about the world of print in such a way as to prevent them from becoming disillusioned with all printed material. One way in which to develop independent, inquiring thinking on the part of readers is to give guided practice in it. The preceding have been but a few of the many ways in which such practice may be offered.

Literary interpretation: reading flexibility

Regardless of the teaching aids and methods used by the literature teacher to develop students' abilities to interpret literature, success is often dependent on students' abilities to read flexibly. Flexibility is necessary for effective comprehension, and comprehension is necessary for interpretation. Literature's infinite variety of form, length, and clarity implies that readers must be capable of varying their reading styles according to their purposes and according to the dictates of the material itself. Yet the quantity of reading required in most literature classes demands that a student be able to read and comprehend all assignments as rapidly as possible. Therefore, the concept of flexibility is one that ought to be incorporated wherever it is applicable. With the wide range of literary types within the province of the teacher of literature, flexibility is a topic that ought to be mentioned often in junior and senior high school literature classes and should probably be introduced to some students in the primary grades, i.e., locating specific stories in readers, and reinforced in grades 4, 5, or 6.

Reading inflexibility produces students who read either fast or slow regardless of their purpose, the demands of the material, or the volume of required reading. Some students fail to comprehend what they read because they read too rapidly to grasp the ideas expressed. (A method that teachers might use to slow down reading rate and increase comprehension is to ask these students to read the material aloud with just enough volume to hear themselves. Research by Collins (1961) indicated that this procedure helps comprehension, and if its effectiveness can be proved to students, they will be likely to incorporate it into their repertoires of reading methods.) However, inflexible readers are more likely to be inflexibly slow than inflexibly fast, and the rate of comprehension tends to decrease unless an effort is made to keep reading rate relatively fast. Teachers, therefore, need ways to teach students to read faster.

Research (Coryell, 1927) has shown that students who read widely have a better attitude toward reading than ones who read less, and one of the primary goals of literature teachers is to produce students who enjoy and practice reading. But students who read slowly rarely read extensively or recreationally, whether by choice or necessity. Grob (1970) noted that both rate of reading and rate of comprehension vary widely from student to student; therefore, a teacher who assigns five typical novels in a year may be asking for a difference in study time that is as high as ninety hours. Obviously the students who are not flexible readers are penalized.

Classroom assignments, however, are not the only frustrations for inflexible readers. Readers who plow through escape fiction at the rate of one hundred words per minute—regardless of whether or not comprehension is exemplary—will take so long to complete what they are reading that they will become discouraged and stop. Moreover, the writing difficulty and style of newspapers, magazines, and fiction on the order of the novels that characteristically head the best seller lists certainly do not warrant the slowest and most inclusive reading of which a person is capable. These conditions, coupled with the fact that we do what we like doing, what we do well, and what we have time to do, bespeak the need to incorporate rate improvement into the teaching of literature reading skills.

Such instruction can be provided through various methods

ranging from teaching machines to study techniques. However, Braam and Berger (1968) indicated that since other methods were equally effective in helping students increase their rates of comprehension, the use of reading machines should be closely questioned. And Berger (1966) included in his research a technique that worked extremely well for the college students in his experiment and which might be tried to equal advantage by teachers at other levels. The method, called "paperback scanning" took the form of providing simple paperback books for students to read at their own rates for five minutes, after which they recorded their rates in words per minute in personal manila folders. This was followed by a training session in which they were directed to scan the pages of the book for very strictly pre-scribed times. The teacher stood before them with a stopwatch counting aloud from one to eight in one-second intervals, then from one to seven, and so on down to intervals of two seconds. Following this, they were skipped back up to ten seconds per page and kept at this rate for two minutes.

After the scanning practice, the students were again asked to read at their own rates, to record their times and rates, and to take another short comprehension test over the materials read.

The times at which students were kept scanning the pages were strictly prescribed for the experiment performed by Berger, but they are probably not critical to the success of the method. The total time of the sessions can probably be quite flexible although the length of scanning time at the beginning and end should be relatively longer than the times of the inter-vening intervals.

An aspect of Berger's study that should also be considered by users of the scanning technique is that he gave students ap-proximately 20 minutes at the conclusion of each scanning ses-sion to read paperback books for enjoyment at their own rates of comprehension.

The previously mentioned record keeping is quite important since it is impossible for a student to feel himself read faster. Another suggestion for successfully implementing this technique is that teachers tape record the presentation of the so-called "countdown." It gets extremely boring for the teacher otherwise, and the taped presentation allows the teacher an opportunity to watch his students or to participate in the procedure himself.

Speculation upon why this has been a successful procedure for increasing flexibility and rate of comprehension leads to the conclusion that it appears to force a reader toward vertical rather than strictly horizontal eye-movement patterns, and it forces him to base his reading on what he is able to see coupled with what he thinks about what he reads. It also forces him to think!

Teachers should try the procedure in various ways. Perhaps, as some have said, ten minutes of the countdown is enough, and although the students in Berger's experiment met for either two or three periods a week, fewer or more meetings might work out better at other levels. It seems most essential that the paperback books be genuinely easy for students to read and that the students be reminded at every stage of the procedure where such types of reading would be appropriate, i.e., escape fiction, newspapers, magazines, etc. It would be a very good idea, also, to couple instruction in increasing rate of comprehension with a presentation of and practice in using a study technique such as Robinson's (1961) Survey, Question, Read, Recite, Review (SQ3R).

SQ3R is a technique designed to help students structure their reading of materials that contain information they must learn. In some respects it can be viewed as an attempt to wean a reader from the help he might expect to receive from a teacher. In Robinson's words

> The SQ3R method . . . consists of five steps: (1) *Survey* the headings and summarize quickly to get the general ideas which will be developed in the assignment, (2) turn the first heading into a *Question,* (3) *Read* the whole section through to answer that question, (4) at the end of the headed section stop to *Recite* from memory on the question and jot the answer down in phrases, (Step 2, 3 and 4 are repeated on each succeeding headed section), and (5) at the end of reading the assignment in this manner then

immediately *Review* the lesson to organize the ideas and recite on the various points to fix them in mind. This higher-level study skill cannot be learned simply by reading about it, it must be practiced under supervision just as with learning any skill. (Robinson, 1961, p. 198)

The use of SQ3R with lessons in increasing rate of comprehension and flexibility appears quite sensible. If after a student has surveyed his reading task and has decided that he already is quite familiar with the material in a given section of it, he can read that section quite rapidly, his purpose being merely to search for information with which he is unfamiliar. His survey may, on the other hand, show him that a slow, close reading of the materials is warranted, and he can then modify his style of reading accordingly.

In all discussions of increasing flexibility it is necessary to point out that students read in order to fulfill the purposes set forth by themselves and by their teachers. Purposes for reading are made known to students either in the form of direct statements that precede their reading or by implication, after they have found that the way they decided to read was inadequate for answering the questions, participating in the discussions, or making the comparisons that followed. Students should be told prior to reading what the teacher's demands will be. Teachers should specify what reading behaviors they think their students should use, provide instruction and time for practice in using them where this seems warranted, and they should help students bridge the gap between a specific type of reading done for a specific work of literature to the general cases in which they will use the same type of reading in the future.

Literary interpretation: critical reading

Perhaps the type of reading most commonly needed for literary interpretation is critical reading. In fact, as it relates to the teacher of literature, critical reading typically takes the form of close reading and interpretation of the various literary forms and involves considerable reading flexibility. But critical reading and critical thinking are inextricably related, and the teacher of literature cannot divorce himself from the other media that his students view and listen to with ever-increasing frequency. Whether his thoughts are on the close reading of poems, or whether he is concerned with the ever-increasing influence of mass advertising or the logic of the typical politician on his students, he finds himself saddled with the responsibility of helping his students improve their ability to read and think critically.

Wolf, King, and Huck (1968) as part of a study designed to teach and measure the effects of teaching critical reading in grades 1 through 6 assembled a list of skills needed by mature readers in the critical reading of informational and persuasive as well as literary material. Their list was then sent to 14 reading experts for validation and/or suggestions for improvement. The revised list is presented below so that teachers can use it along with their other understandings of reading comprehension to plan discussions, essay questions, reading activities, and other exercises or materials used in the teaching of critical reading.

Skills identified for critical reading:

I. Analysis and evaluation of informational and persuasive material
   A. Semantics in writing
      1. Distinguishing between vague and precise words.
      2. Recognizing the difference between connotative and denotative meanings of words.
      3. Recognizing the persuasive use of words through such devices as: name calling, glittering generalities, and plain folks.
      4. Evaluating the effectiveness of the use of words according to the author's purpose.
   B. Logic in writing
      1. Recognizing and evaluating the validity of writing.
         a. Examining the validity of an argument, i.e., judging whether conclusions necessarily follow from premises.
         b. Classifying into groups and sub-groups.
         c. Determining appropriate use of all, some, and none statements.
         d. Discovering unstated premises and conclusions.
      2. Recognizing and evaluating the reliability of printed materials.

      a. Discovering ways to test the reliability of information.

      b. Determining soundness of premises and conclusions.

      c. Detecting material fallacies, e.g., hasty generalizations, unrepresentative generalizations, faulty causal generalizations, *post hoc* reasoning, false analogies, false dilemmas, fallacies of composition and division, and all or nothing statements.

      d. Recognizing illogical reasoning in persuasive writing, e.g., testimonial, identification and transfer, band wagon, card stacking.

      e. Recognizing and evaluating different forms of informational and persuasive writing.

      f. Distinguishing between objective and subjective evidence.

      g. Judging the reliability of information.

   C. Authenticity of writing

      1. Recognizing adequacy of information or the necessity of suspending judgment.

      2. Comparing relevant information from multiple sources to recognize agreement or contradiction.

      3. Recognizing authoritative sources and evaluating them according to established criteria.

      4. Evaluating the qualifications of the author.

      5. Recognizing the publisher and sponsor's commitments.

II. Analysis and evaluation of literary material

   A. Literary forms

      1. Recognizing characteristics of various genre of fiction, such as: fantasy, realistic fiction, historical fiction, and biography.

      2. Distinguishing among variants of a particular form of fiction. For example, distinguishing between various forms of fantasy: make-believe, fairy tale, folk tale, modern fantasy, fable, myth, science fiction, allegory.

      3. Developing criteria for evaluating each type of fiction.

      4. Recognizing the characteristic forms of poetry, e.g., narrative, lyric, haiku.

      5. Developing criteria for evaluating poetry.

   B. Components of literature

      1. Identifying and evaluating characterization.

      a. Distinguishing between character delineation and character development.
      b. Recognizing ways the author reveals character.
      c. Developing criteria for assessing characterization.
      d. Comparing and evaluating methods of character development in two books.

  2. Identifying and evaluating plot structure.
      a. Recognizing the structure of the plot: accumulative, episodic, parallel.
      b. Tracing the development of plot structure: the sequence, the climax, dénouement.
      c. Recognizing ways of attaining the climax: suspense, surprise, size and color of pictures.
      d. Recognizing and evaluating effectiveness of special techniques of plot development: foreshadowing and flashback.

  3. Identifying and evaluating setting.
      a. Recognizing the elements of setting: place, time.
      b. Understanding the relationship of setting to action and character development.

  4. Identifying and evaluating theme.
      a. Distinguishing between theme and plot in a story.
      b. Identifying the story theme and comparing themes in several books.
      c. Evaluating effectiveness of theme presentation.

C. Literary devices
  1. Identifying and evaluating author's use of language.
      a. Interpreting and evaluating figurative language: metaphor, simile, personification.
      b. Evaluating the use of dialogue and authentic speech.
      c. Evaluating the author's style of writing.
      d. Interpreting symbolism and judging its effectiveness.

  2. Identifying and evaluating mood of writing.
      a. Recognizing the mood of selected poems and stories.
      b. Recognizing different ways the author achieves humor: surprise, slap-stick, exaggerations, anachronism.

       c. Recognizing the effective use of satire or irony.
3. Identifying and evaluating point of view.
       a. Recognizing the point of view from which the story is told.
       b. Considering how the story would be different if told from another point of view.
       c. Comparing books written from different points of view. (Wolf, King, and Huck, 1968, pp. 450-52)

This list exemplifies the complexity of critical reading; it also indicates its importance in the literature classroom. It is through critical reading that understanding is achieved. It is through critical reading that literary appreciation develops.

The appreciation of literature: comprehension

A student's capacity to appreciate literature is directly related to his ability to comprehend what he reads, and the concept of reading comprehension is so complicated that even though definitive research has not been done on it, there is not space enough in this paper to deal adequately with the research that has been done. Davis (1968), for example, isolated eight discrete subskills within the general category of comprehension: remembering word meanings, inferring word meanings from context, understanding content, weaving ideas in the content, making inferences about the content, recognizing the author's tone, mood, and purpose, identifying the author's literary techniques, and following the structure of the content. These eight subskills must be described in some detail before knowing them can be of practical value in planning lessons, but this list is of value to caution teachers not to oversimplify the concept of comprehension and to encourage them to place proper emphasis on it in the literature classroom.

The appreciation of literature: growth

Comprehension, however, is only the basis for literary appreciation. Early (1960) described three stages in a pupil's growth in literary appreciation: unconscious enjoyment, self-conscious appreciation, and conscious delight. She described a reader as moving along a continuum from liking certain types of literature but not knowing why, to a stage in which he is willing to exert considerable effort: to discover why events are happening, to search for well-formed characters rather than stereotypes, and to appreciate psychological rather than physical conflicts; to the stage where he responds with delight, knows why, chooses discriminatingly, and relies on his own judgment. It is hoped that the suggestions offered in this paper will assist teachers in finding ways to help students move from the lower to the higher stages of appreciation.

Literary appreciation: the taxonomy of the affective domain

A concept similar to Early's (1960) evolution of literary appreciation is found in a taxonomy of educational objectives for the affective domain (cf. Krathwohl, Bloom, and Masia, 1964). Even though the various levels have not been totally verified through research, it is suggested that teachers examine the existing taxonomy in order to structure their thoughts as well as their teaching procedures with the idea of helping students move toward the higher levels of the taxonomy in their regard for literature study. A skeleton of the progression the authors think is reasonable in the development of affect is contained in the following quotation:

> . . . the continuum progress(es) from a level at which the individual is merely *aware* of a phenomenon, being able to perceive it. At the next level he is *willing to attend* to phenomena. At the next level he *responds* to the phenomena with a *positive feeling*. Eventually he may feel strongly enough to go *out of his* way to respond. At some point in the process he conceptualizes his behavior and feelings and *organizes* these conceptualizations into a structure. This structure grows in complexity as *it becomes his life outlook.* (Krathwohl, Bloom, and Masia, 1964, p. 27)

Although it is quite possible that final analysis of this structuring of growth in affect may not hold up in actual practice, it will be interesting for teachers to substitute things such as "desire to actively seek out and read good books" for "phenomena" in the quoted paragraph and then to examine classroom procedures with an idea of determining whether they help or hinder the progress of students along the continuum.

Questions for further research

It is not known with any degree of certainty what effect the reading of literature has upon readers, and there has as yet been but little research on this question. Shirley (1969) and Neal (1968) are representative of beginnings, but much more needs to be done. It is not known what "appreciation" is all about, and it is not known whether the taxonomy of the affective domain is a real taxonomy, that is, whether the levels are ordered, or whether there should be more or fewer levels. Research should be addressed to verifying this document, and then attempts should be made to develop diagnostic and evaluative instruments to discover where a student stands regarding the appreciation of literature. The semantic differential seems a possibility for parts of such diagnoses, but there has not been enough research in literature to tell whether it really possesses this potential. Methods of teaching literature have not been adequately researched. Studies such as those of Hosic (1921) and Coryell (1927), previously cited, have not been replicated on present-day students using this generation's teachers, and their conclusions must, therefore, remain suspect for that reason. The same is true of the studies of Richards (1929) and Squire (1964). They are excellent research documents, but they are restricted to times, groups of students, and literary selections that cannot be termed representative of the wide range for which information is lacking. These studies should be replicated.

It is not really known what reading comprehension is all about, and attempts to improve students' abilities in it are therefore predicated on unverified bases. The U. S. Office of Education-supported Targeted Research and Development Program on Reading, which is using the Convergence Technique (first advocated for use in cancer research) to analyze the reading process and design instructional procedures to teach it effectively, will offer a model of the reading process as one of its by-products. It will be of value for teachers and researchers to use this model to increase their awareness of what is actually involved when reader and writing are brought together.

Although much research still needs to be done and many questions need to be answered, classroom teachers should have sufficient preparation to teach effectively. Presumably, the large numbers of college literature courses that most teachers of literature have taken have provided them with insights into how skilled, mature readers read literature. Moreover, methods courses, courses in children's and adolescent literature, and regular perusals of professional publications have presumably acquainted them with appropriate materials to teach. Educational psychology courses have supposedly imparted knowledge of children's psychological development, so they are relatively skilled in choosing methods and materials appropriate for the mental capacities and emotional needs of the students with whose instruction they have been entrusted.

Teachers, then, should be able to survey the literature that is available, analyze the specific needs and capabilities of their students, choose the literary selections that are most suitable for teaching these students, and prepare their lessons. If the school system that has hired a teacher has adopted a literature anthology for use with his classes, then he has given up or has been forced to give up the first of his choices to the compilers of the anthology and to the administrator or curriculum committee who purchased it.

If he follows without question or modification the suggestions in his teacher's manual or his school district's curriculum guide for teaching the works that have been anthologized, then he has relinquished or has been forced to relinquish the second of his choices. If he is also ignorant of the fact that some of his students do not like the selections he has asked them to read and have failed to learn the material he has taught them, he has forgotten or ignored the information he supposedly assimilated during his educational psychology courses.

If he knows literature, knows methods and materials, knows

the characteristics of students, and has the freedom to teach as he believes he should and is still dissatisfied with his accomplishments and those of his students, it may be that what he (or his supervisor) needs is a course in the teaching of reading.

References

Ames, W. S. The development of a classification scheme of contextual aids. *Reading Research Quarterly*, 1966, *2*, 57-82.

Ames, W. S. The use of classification schemes in teaching the use of contextual aids. *Journal of Reading*, 1970, *14*, 5-8, 50.

Andresen, O. Evaluating the author's theme in literature. In Robinson, H. A., and Rauch, S. J. (Eds.) *Corrective reading in the high school classroom: perspectives in reading no. 6.* Newark, Delaware: International Reading Association, 1966, 64-74.

Andrews, L. Author biography and poetry study. *Research in the Teaching of English*, 1970, *4*, 37-44.

Berger, A. Effectiveness of four methods of increasing reading rate, comprehension, and flexibility. Unpublished doctoral dissertation, Syracuse University, 1966.

Braam, L. S., and Berger, A. Effectiveness of four methods of increasing reading rate, comprehension, and flexibility. *Journal of Reading*, 1968, *11*, 346-52.

Collins, R. The comprehension of prose materials by college freshmen when read silently and when read aloud. *Journal of Educational Research*, 1961, *55*, 79-82.

Coryell, Nancy G. *An evaluation of extensive and intensive teaching of literature.* New York: Bureau of Publications, Teachers College, Columbia University, 1927.

Davis, F. B. Research in comprehension in reading. *Reading Research Quarterly*, 1968, *3*, 499-545.

Deighton, L. C. *Vocabulary development in the classroom.* New York: Bureau of Publications, Teachers College, Columbia University, 1959.

Early, Margaret J. Stages of growth in literary appreciation. *English Journal*, 1960, *49*, 161-67.

Farrell, E. J. Listen, my children, and you shall read. . . . *English Journal*, 1966, *55*, 39-45, 68.

Frost, R. *The poetry of Robert Frost*, E. C. Lathem (Ed.). New York: Holt, Rinehart and Winston, 1969.

Frost, R. *Complete poems of Robert Frost.* New York: Holt, Rinehart and Winston, 1964.

Gallo, D. R. The construction and validation of an instrument to assess teachers' opinions of methods of teaching poetry to tenth grade students of average ability. Unpublished doctoral dissertation, Syracuse University, 1968.

Grob, J. A. Reading rate and study-time demands on secondary students. *Journal of Reading*, 1970, *13*, 285-88, 316.

Herber, H. L. *Success with words . . . in social studies, English, science, mathematics.* New York: Scholastic Book Services, 1964.

Herber, H. L. *Teaching reading in content areas.* Englewood Cliffs, New Jersey: Prentice-Hall, 1970.

Hosic, J. F. *Empirical studies in school reading.* New York: Teachers College, Columbia University, 1921.

Huus, Helen. Development of taste in literature in the elementary grades. *Elementary English*, 1962, *39*, 780-89 and 1963, *40*, 56-67.

Joll, L. W. Development of taste in literature in the junior high school. *Elementary English*, 1963, *40*, 183-88, 217.

Krathwohl, D. R., Bloom, B. S., and Masia, B. B. *Taxonomy of educational objectives, handbook II: affective domain.* New York: David McKay, 1964.

Livingston, H. The effects of general semantics on responses to a poem. *Research in the Teaching of English*, 1969, *3*, 25-29.

Martin, B. In defense of literary encounter. In Bracken, Dorothy K. Literature for children. *The Reading Teacher*, 1968, *22*, 187-91.

Neal, Carolyn M. Sex differences in personality and reading ability. *Journal of Reading*, 1968, *11*, 609-14, 633.

Petty, W. T., Herold, C. P., and Stoll, Earline. *The state of knowledge about the teaching of vocabulary.* Champaign, Illinois: National Council of Teachers of English, 1968.

Purves, A. C. You can't teach Hamlet, he's dead. *English Journal*, 1968, *57*, 832-36.

Quealy, R. J. Senior high school students' use of contextual aids in reading. *Reading Research Quarterly*, 1969, *4*, 512-33.

Quinn, Sister M. Bernetta. Symbolic landscape in Frost's "Nothing Gold Can Stay." *English Journal*, 1966, *55*, 621-24.

Reid, J. M. An adventure in programing literature. *English Journal*, 1963, *52*, 659-73.

Richards, I. A. *Practical criticism: a study of literary judgment.* New York: Harcourt, Brace and World, 1929.

Robinson, F. P. Study skills for superior students in secondary schools. *The Reading Teacher*, 1961, *15*, 29-33, 37. Reprinted in Karlin, R. *Teaching reading in high school: selected articles.* New York: Bobbs-Merrill, 1969.

Rottenberg, Annette T. "Obviously bad." *English Journal*, 1963, *52*, 496-500.

Sargent, Eileen E., Huus, Helen, and Andresen, O. *How to read a book*. Mangrum, C. T. (Ed.) Reading aids series. Newark, Delaware: International Reading Association, 1970.

Shirley, F. L. The influence of reading on concepts, attitudes, and behavior. *Journal of Reading,* 1969, *12,* 369-72, 407-13.

Smith, Helen K. The responses of good and poor readers when asked to read for different purposes. *Reading Research Quarterly,* 1967, *3,* 53-88.

Smith, Nila B. *American reading instruction.* New York: Silver Burdett, 1934.

Sparke, W., and McKowen, C. *Montage: investigations in language.* Macmillan, 1970.

Squire, J. R. *The responses of adolescents while reading four short stories.* Champaign, Illinois: National Council of Teachers of English, 1964.

Squire, J. R., and Applebee, R. K. *High school English instruction today.* New York: Appleton-Century Crofts, 1968.

Vine, H. A., Vine, Janet D., and Jewett, A. *Reading guide and review tests: discovering literature.* Boston: Houghton Mifflin, 1968.

Vine, H. A., *et al. Teaching reading in secondary schools.* Syracuse, New York: School of Education, Syracuse University, 1967.

Vine, H.A., *et al. Reading guide and review tests: exploring literature.* Boston: Houghton Mifflin, 1968.

Weekes, Blanche. *The influence of meaning on children's choices of poetry.* New York: Bureau of Publications, Teachers College, Columbia University, 1929.

Wilson, J. R. *Responses of college freshmen to three novels.* Champaign, Illinois: National Council of Teachers of English, 1966.

Wolf, Willavene, King, Martha L., and Huck, Charlotte S. Teaching critical reading to elementary school children. *Reading Research Quarterly,* 1968, *3,* 435-98.

Clyde G. Corle

Reading in mathematics:
A review of recent research

This paper reviews the research on reading and mathematics in the elementary school. It focuses on the arithmetic concepts and the reading skills necessary to mathematical achievement and to the relationship between the two. It also considers the attendant problem of selecting text materials appropriate to the students' reading levels.

In order to provide the reader with current research, only studies published after 1950 are included. Because of the volume of material dealing with reading and mathematics in the elementary grades, no attempt has been made to provide a comprehensive survey of all related materials. Rather, the studies selected are cited as examples of major research findings on the subject.

These findings have led to the development of the thesis that mathematicians are in reality specialists in the art of communication. They express numerical ideas in precise symbolic notation, and they use language that bridges cultural and social differences. The conversations of small children show continuous interchange of quantitative information. Alert teachers include mathematical vocabulary in primary reading word lists, and they encourage young children to practice the communication skills that are necessary for exchanging quantitative ideas.

An important objective of any elementary teacher is to teach skills for reading in the content areas. Texts and reference books convey information about the phenomena of quantitative relationships. Printed resource materials provide precise statements of number properties, and they suggest certain algorithms to be followed in the computational operations. Teachers depend upon reading skills when verbal problems are assigned, when they give directions, and when they measure the achievement of the learners. For those reasons, competence in reading is an important consideration for success in learning mathematics. By the same logic, since mathematical language is one of the components of a complete vocabulary, no pupil can achieve success in reading unless he can read understandingly in the mathematical content area.

Arithmetic concepts necessary for mathematical achievement

Research has shown that in order to succeed in mathematics —in fact, even to understand it—a pupil must possess certain capacities. Prominent among the researchers who have worked to identify these capacities is Piaget.[1] He postulated that a prerequisite to understanding mathematics is conservation. Piaget (1953) contended that a child does not acquire the notion of number or of other mathematical relationships through the verbalizations of a teacher. He develops understanding only when his mental maturity is sufficient to grasp the principle of conservation of quantity. The child then can see that the number of items in a group remains the same no matter how they are arranged. Any adult attempt to impose mathematical concepts on a child prematurely results in verbal learning only; in short, the child learns the names of numbers and pseudoconcepts which are not based on rational understanding (e.g., Flavell, 1963, 313, 315). Thus, the first prerequisite to the development of mathematical capacity is the achievement of conservation. In fact, Piaget (1965) stated that the conservation of quantity, weight, volume, length, etc. is a necessary condition for all rational activity.[2] It is a logical concept rather than a nu-

---

[1]Piaget is primarily a researcher, and while he has written voluminously, much of his work is in French. A great part of it has not been translated. However, J. H. Flavell's (1963) book *The Developmental Psychology of Jean Piaget* provides an excellent English interpretation of Piaget's theory and work prior to 1960.

[2]See also Almy (1966).

merical notion (Piaget, 1953). Piaget has also insisted that conservation is necessary to an understanding of cardinal number.

Piaget's theory of conservation was supported in a study by Brace and Nelson (1966) which found a positive relationship between five- and six-year-old children's knowledge of cardinal number and their ability to conserve number. The relationship decreased with age, and the conservation skills of children from high socioeconomic backgrounds were significantly better than those of children with low socioeconomic backgrounds.

Piaget's concept of conservation of length was studied by Murray (1965). Murray's report concurred that the transition from nonconservation to conservation of length occurs sometime between the ages of seven and eight. Any training procedures prior to this transition age appeared only to result in memorization of statements about the abstractions rather than to provide an awareness of the meanings of the relationships themselves.

Another of Piaget's mathematical prerequisites is his concept of reversibility. This concept is closely related to that of conservation, and it necessitates an understanding of the fact that invariance of quantity is insured by the possibility of an inverse transformation back to the original state. Regardless of how the quantity is manipulated, it can by an inverse action be restored to its original state (e.g., $5 - 2 = 3$, $3 + 2 = 5$; $10 \times 5 = 50$, $50 \div 5 = 10$). Until a child develops the capability to perceive such relationships, he cannot succeed in mathematics.

Murray (1968) again researched Piaget's theory in terms of cognitive conflict and reversibility training. His subjects were 119 pupils from kindergarten through second grade. For this group, the transition from nonconservers to conservers seemed to occur between the ages of six and seven, somewhat earlier than the age indicated by Piaget and by Murray's earlier work.

Almy (1966), using five- to eight-year-olds, studied the age at which her students attained reversibility. Contrary to Murray's findings, Almy's study showed that the age of reversibility for most of her middle-class second graders was seven years and four months. Her findings supported those of Piaget concerning the maturational development of a child's logical abilities.

Each of the above prerequisites contributes to a child's concept of number. According to Piaget, number is essentially a synthesis of two logical entities: class and asymmetrical relation. Cardinal numbers denote a set of objects and treat them as though they are all alike. Ordinal numbers, however, arrange the objects in relation to each other; then they denote them in a sequence. The ordination process involves an understanding of relation rather than class; it creates a set of asymmetrical relations. Therefore, numerical units are both class elements and asymmetrical elements at the same time. The child must understand that in order to count them, they must be counted seriatim. Once counted, they are again just a particular quantity of objects. Thus, before a child can succeed in mathematics, he must understand cardinal numbers, ordinal numbers, and their interrelationships. The capacities necessary to accomplish this are a result of attaining a certain level of mental maturity.

It should be noted, however, that not all researchers have reached full agreement with Piaget's maturational concepts. A major exception is Bruner,[3] who has stated that a child's environment can be changed so that it is consistent with his intellectual development.

Bruner's (1960) statement, "We begin with the hypothesis that any subject can be taught in some intellectually honest form to any child at any stage of development," has provoked numerous protests. Kline (1966) proposed that ". . . what can happen and does happen when this doctrine is taken too seriously . . . [is that] students accept the abstraction docilely and are as understanding and as critical . . . as when they learn a catechism."

---

[3]Bruner's basic research was completed in 1956 when he published the results of an experiment with Harvard undergraduates. He classified thinking strategies in the following manner: systematic evaluation, a process of concept attainment, regression to the familiar in attacking a problem, reluctance to use negative instances, and a preference for common elements or conjunctive concepts. Since 1956, Bruner's work has consisted chiefly of interpretative reviews of the studies of other researchers. His *Study of Thinking*, however, has remained a classic in psychological research.

When the above statement was made by Bruner, he was serving as the recorder for the Woods Hole Conference, and *The Process of Education* was the report of that conference. The statement that provoked so much discussion might have been Bruner's own, or it might have been the consensus of Cronbach, Page, and a number of other members of the conference.

Piaget himself recognized the importance of environment in the development of cognitive functions. He cited three steps in this development:

a] The adaptation of an organism to its environment during its growth, together with the interactions and autoregulations which characterize the development of the "epigenetic system."

b] The adaptation of intelligence in the course of the construction of its own structures, which depends as much on progressive internal coordinations as on information acquired through experience.

c] The establishment of cognitive or more generally, epistemological relations, which consist neither of a simple copy of external objects nor of a mere unfolding performed inside the subject, but rather involve a set of structures progressively constructed by continuous interaction between the subject and the external world. (1970, p. 703)

Perhaps Bruner and his followers are saying the same thing. Certainly both Bruner and Piaget recognize the importance of a developmental sequence. Where Piaget focuses upon maturational changes, Bruner asks, "How can the environment be changed to be consistent with a child's general development?" The question is not one of "either-or," whether we support Piaget or Bruner. It is foolish in elementary education to ignore developmental traits. It is equally as foolish to argue that nothing in the child's nurture contributes to his intellectual development. Piaget's observations have established a considerable age-range for the development of the intellectual behaviors of children. Bruner believes that environmental facts may modify the learning rate of a given individual. It is doubtful whether there is actually any real difference between the two positions. In any case, teachers of mathematics should consider both maturation and environment when they present arithmetical concepts to their students.

The relationship of reading skills to mathematical achievement

Research has shown that numerical concepts alone will not guarantee success in mathematics. This is especially true in the area of written, or verbal, arithmetic problems. The ability to compute correct answers to these problems is directly related to the ability to read and to interpret them.

Corle and Coulter (1964) identified the reading skills which enable intermediate-grade children to interpret verbal arithmetic problems as: 1] vocabulary development, 2] literal interpretation of the problem, and 3] reasoning—the selection of the proper solution process.

The importance of vocabulary development was emphasized by Fay (1965) and by Vanderlinde (1964). Fay noted that while success in mathematics depends on a child's understanding of the number system, it also depends on a vocabulary of terms which provide a basis for mathematical reasoning and clues for the use of numerical processes. Vanderlinde stated that students who do not comprehend the technical vocabulary used in a content area do not comprehend the important ideas within that area. These writers seem to agree that the study of the technical vocabulary of mathematics is an essential part of the program.

Data collected by Vanderlinde (1964) and by Lyda and Duncan (1967) indicated that the direct study of quantitative vocabulary produced a significant growth in elementary students' problem-solving abilities.

The importance of literal interpretation of the problem statement was supported by Chase (1961) who found that ability to note details in reading problems was a skill necessary for success in verbal problems.

The importance of selecting the proper solution process for

a verbal problem has been treated by Cathcart and Liedtke (1969), Wilson (1967), Stern and Keislar (1967), Stern (1967), and Irish (1964). Cathcart and Liedtke studied the difference in mathematical success between reflective students and impulsive students. The researchers hypothesized that reflective students would be more successful because they would reflect upon the quality of their answers; the impulsive students would give unconsidered responses. The findings indicated that the reflective students did achieve better scores than the impulsive ones in problem solving and in recalling basic facts, but not in mathematical understanding. The data in this study also indicated that children become more reflective as their age increases.

Wilson (1967), who distributed 54 fourth graders evenly over three treatment groups (action-sequence, wanted-given, and practice only), found that the wanted-given treatment produced significantly greater success with verbal problems than either of the other two. He also reported that the action-sequence structures of direct problems inhibited the choice of correct operations for indirect problems.

Stern and Keislar (1967) studied the effect of instruction in problem-solving strategy upon third graders' abilities to interpret verbal problems. They found that children who were taught strategies for solving problems performed better with new, but similar, problems than children who had not been given such instruction.

In a followup study, Stern (1967) tested two strategy programs for teaching verbal problem interpretation to third graders. She tested her hypotheses under two conditions of verbalization—not speaking and speaking—and concluded that young children can be taught strategies which will improve their ability to solve certain kinds of problems. A simple strategy was more effective 1] with the age group used in the study and 2] with familiar materials. No reliable differences were evident when overt verbalizations were used as opposed to nonspeaking. In a somewhat similar study, Irish (1964) reported that her fourth graders spent 10 per cent of their arithmetic instructional time in stating verbal generalizations appropriate to the topic under study. Contrary to Stern's conclusions about verbalization, Irish found that the experimental children made significantly greater average growth in problem solving and in computation than the children who did not receive this training.

The foregoing studies appear to point out two elements necessary for pupils to learn how to compute verbal problems. First is a familiarity with words and expressions used in the specific area in which the problem occurs. Second, the learner must become familiar with certain systematic procedures which lead to logical consideration of all of the elements which contribute to the solution of the problem. Problem-solving effectiveness will not emerge from casual or isolated instruction in either or both of these elements. Vocabulary functions best when teacher-pupil interaction creates a need for the right word in expressing an idea. Familiarity with systematic strategies grows out of group problem solving, trial and error efforts by the learners, and group success in developing acceptable solutions. (Corle and Coulter, 1964)

A final skill for which research has suggested a relationship to mathematical success is listening. Although only two studies considered all three skills—reading, mathematics, and listening —among the variables being studied, it seems that some mention should be made of the possible relationship—especially when the emphasis on listening as it relates to reading success is considered. Stull (1964) studied the effect of tape-recorded readings of verbal arithmetic problems, played while intermediate-grade children read the problems silently. He concluded that there was no significant difference between problem solvers who listened to the readings and those who did not listen except on one of the subtests: the "listeners" were more capable of recognizing missing or unavailable information than those who received no such assistance.

Cleland and Toussaint (1962) stated that listening, intelligence, and arithmetic computation ability should all be considered in making estimates of reading potential. Such a relationship between listening and reading infers a relationship, through reading, between listening and mathematics. Auditory stimuli seem to provide many of the necessary concepts for success in mathematics; clearly there is a definite need for further research in listening as a tool for mathematics teachers.

Problem solving in mathematics

There seems to be general agreement among researchers that certain mathematical capabilities and certain reading skills are necessary for success in mathematics. Although the research previously cited has dealt primarily with these abilities independent of each other, they have also been studied together as factors contributing to mathematical achievement.

Chase (1960) studied 15 variables which might affect an intermediate-grade pupil's ability to solve verbal problems. He concluded that the ability to compute, skill in noting details in reading, and a knowledge of fundamental arithmetic concepts were the three major predictors of problem-solving ability. Chase also noted the importance of a knowledge of generalizations which underlie the number system and the ability to apply reading skills to a variety of purposes.

Balow (1964) studied the role of reading and computation as determinants of problem-solving ability and found that both had an effect on the success of 468 sixth graders with verbal problems.

Glennon and Callahan (1968), after reviewing a number of studies on research in problem solving, concluded that the following four factors were most important for success: 1] general reading skills, including vocabulary; 2] problem-solving reading skills, including comprehension of the problem statement, selection of relevant details, and selection of the proper solution procedure; 3] mechanical computation and a mathematical understanding of the concept of quantity, the number system, and important arithmetic relationships; and 4] a spatial factor, involving the ability to visualize and conceptualize objects and symbols in more than one dimension and to use mental imagery to clarify word meanings.

Other researchers have gone beyond mathematics and reading abilities and have studied the effects of other variables upon a child's problem-solving ability. They have identified such factors as motor and verbal abilities (Cawley and Goodman, 1968), attitudes and personality characteristics (Ross, 1964), physical condition and disease (Ross, 1964), and IQ (Balow, 1964; Chase, 1961; and Cawley and Goodman, 1968). Although it is not the purpose of this paper to discuss these variables in detail, each is a factor which should be considered in evaluating a student's success with reading and arithmetic.

In addition to studies of pupil-related variables which affect mathematical performance, there are also studies of materials-related variables. Williams and McCreight (1965) studied the effect of question placement—first or last—on 220 fifth- and sixth-graders' success with verbal problems. Their findings indicated that although there was no significant difference in performance as a result of question placement, there was interaction between question placement and 1] arithmetic achievement and 2] time required for problem solving. High achievers did better when the question was placed first, and problem-solving time was less when the question was first.

Burns and Yonally (1964), using fourth and fifth graders, tried different ways of ordering the data needed to solve the problems. They concluded that 1] pupils are less successful in getting correct answers when the numerical data are not in the order needed and 2] arithmetic reasoning ability is positively related to the ability to solve problems which present the numerical data in mixed order.

Textbook readability

The problems of format and their relationship to success in mathematics emphasize the importance of careful textbook selection. The textbook has always been an important tool for teachers of elementary mathematics; in fact, it is often the only resource provided for mathematics instruction. Reys and Knowles (1968) surveyed the status of elementary school textbooks and found that 66 per cent of the schools used one textbook while 26 per cent used two. Such dependence upon textbooks underscores the importance of giving consideration to the difficulty of the vocabulary and the nonverbal items such as graphs used in them and to the interest that they hold for students.

Among these three readability factors, major research emphasis has been placed on the study of vocabulary. This study divides into analyses of the two kinds of vocabulary which appear in mathematics texts: general and quantitative. Kerfoot (1961), Repp (1960), and Johnson (1952) are among the researchers who have investigated the general vocabulary difficulty of elementary arithmetic textbooks. Kerfoot examined six first- and second-grade books and developed a list of words which were found in at least three books and which were used at least 10 times. These words were checked against the *Dale List of 769 Easy Words* and the *Revised Gates List of Vocabulary for the Primary Grades*. He concluded that the list he had prepared represented a selection of words which a child is likely to meet in his first or second year of mathematics instruction. Therefore, if the teacher knows in advance what vocabulary is needed for comprehension in arithmetic, he can introduce those words which are not yet a part of the child's vocabulary. Reading instruction in anticipated vocabulary may reduce the reading problem and may thus contribute to the understanding of arithmetic concepts.

Repp (1960) tabulated 3,329 words taken from five texts widely used at the third-grade level and found that from 1,379 to 2,096 words were new to third graders. Johnson (1952) concluded that the 684 fifth graders used in her study needed a program of word enrichment to deal with the vocabulary in their textbooks and lesson materials.

Kolson (1963) and Reed (1965) both studied quantitative vocabulary. Kolson concluded that of the 229 arithmetic words used by the kindergartners that he studied, 70 per cent were quantitative words. Reed found no significant agreement between the mathematics vocabulary (textbook and otherwise) and the vocabulary in the reading series used by her pupils. She also found greater, but not significant, agreement between the mathematics vocabulary and standard word lists.

Another factor, closely related to vocabulary, which affects textbook readability is the use of nonverbal items such as symbols, formulae, graphs, and diagrams. Johnson (1957)[4] included them as sources of reading difficulty in his study of mathematics textbooks, but other research on the topic was not found. There is no question that the modern approach to mathematics has increased the volume of symbol usage in children's instructional materials. Therefore, an important consideration for needed research must be the topic of nonverbal items in elementary school mathematics.

Although this paper will not present a defense of textbooks as a tool of instruction in mathematics, there is not any question that they are used extensively. As a result, there is concern that the nonverbal items included be appropriate to the students' abilities. There is considerable evidence that vocabulary specialists have discovered a disproportionate number of unfamiliar words in the mathematics books used by young children. Kerfoot has expressed his belief that teaching the vocabulary which children need to learn information in any content area is actually a function of the reading teacher.

Given this situation, it becomes obvious that some measure of textbook readability is important. The most common measurement technique currently in use is the readability formula, which is primarily concerned with the difficulty of the text. Among the researchers using this technique are Heddens and Smith (1964) who used the Spache and the Dale-Chall formulas to study five commercial texts. The Spache formula was used for the primary texts (grades 1-3) and the Dale-Chall formula was used for intermediate texts (grades 4-6). These researchers concluded that all of the five textbooks series showed readability levels above the assigned grade level. The books varied in reading level from text to text as well as within sec-

---

[4]The Johnson study, conducted at the secondary level, was included in this paper because of the lack of elementary-level studies on this topic.

tions of the same text. Obviously inconsistency such as that reported is a handicap for many learners, particularly those who find reading difficult.

Vocabulary and nonverbal factors, however, are not the only consideration to be used in textbook evaluation. Within the last few years, emphasis has been broadened to include not only the difficulty of the text, but also the interest that it holds for the student. Faison (1951) reported a study of the readability of all textbooks, grades five through eight, which compared both the level of difficulty and the interest potential of 38 texts. He concluded that the mathematics books ranked the hardest to read and next to the lowest in interest.

Summary

The major points which were emphasized in this review of research are as follows:

1] Certain intellectual capabilities are essential for mathematical achievement. According to Piaget these are competence with the concept of conservation—of number, quantity, length, volume, and weight; the achievement of the concept of reversibility; and the maturation of logical abilities. Piaget stated that a child must be able to comprehend the fact that a number is the synthesis of two logical entities: class and asymmetrical relations, before he can achieve in mathematics. He contended that these capabilities are achieved when a child has matured sufficiently to comprehend them.

Bruner, while accepting a developmental sequence in mathematical capability, contended that a child's environment can be changed so that it is consistent with his intellectual development. Piaget allowed considerable age-range for the development of the intellectual behaviors of children, and Bruner believed that environmental factors modify the learning rate of a child. Perhaps these amount to the same concept. In any event, both maturation and environment should be considered by teachers of elementary mathematics.

2] Certain reading skills are necessary to success in solving verbal arithmetic problems. According to Corle and Coulter, the three most important reading skills are vocabulary development, literal interpretation of the problem, and selection of the proper solution process (reasoning). It is also noted that listening skills seem to be related to mathematical ability, primarily through their relationship to reading achievement.

3] Success in mathematical problem solving is greatly influenced by certain mathematical prerequisites and reading skills, but it is also affected by other variables. Among these are motor abilities, verbal abilities, personality characteristics, and physical conditions. It is also influenced by the arrangement of data within a mathematics problem.

4] Textbook readability is a major consideration in a child's mathematical success, because in many classrooms textbooks are the only resource provided for mathematics instruction. Therefore, the vocabulary, both general and quantitative, the difficulty of nonverbal items such as symbols and graphs, and the interest level of the text should be evaluated carefully to insure that the material is suitable to the child's ability and grade level.

The above-mentioned points not only indicate the current state of research on teaching reading in the mathematics classroom, but they also have implications for future research.

Suggestions for further research

When a reader attempts to study the research in a particular area of educational effort, he is sometimes overwhelmed by the countless reports he must review. He begins to believe that there should be a moratorium on educational studies, certainly until all of the current ones have been read, classified, and evaluated. However, as one after another passes over the desk, certain gaps, inadequacies, and omissions appear. The reviewer begins to notice critical areas which have been overlooked or ignored by researchers in that field. Perhaps that is why educators feel that there is a never-ending need for competent research in the content areas of education.

This reviewer undertook to study research reports that bring into focus two important elementary subjects, reading and arithmetic. He examined several hundred studies whose titles suggested some kind of possible relationship, but found little that could bring a fresh point of view to an inquiring teacher of elementary children. What appeared to be missing were specific studies that explained the effect of certain teaching strategies in one subject area on the learning achievement in another. To be more specific, this author has identified several areas in which only limited research information was available:

1] Mathematical language is one of the components of a complete reading vocabulary. Should reading instruction cover the entire range of reading competence, or should mathematics teachers assume the responsibility for developing the language in their own way?

2] Numerous studies are available which show interest in Piaget's work with preschool and early primary children. A search for studies dealing with preadolescent and early adolescent children in relation to Piaget's theories was less fruitful.

3] Studies which have opened the subject of the effect of democratic interaction on verbal problem solving have been limited. Will the use of class discussions of mathematical problem situations affect the ability of children to make independently correct interpretations of verbal problems?

4] Listening—or auditory stimuli—have always been among the teaching tools used by good teachers.

Very few studies of the effects of listening as a mathematical teaching strategy were found.

5] A survey of the advertising literature issued by textbook publishers in support of their products revealed very little information about the readability and the interest appeal of their books. Current studies, either by educators or by publishers, appear to be in short supply.

6] This reviewer found very few studies which reported investigations into techniques for teaching symbols, formulae, graphs, diagrams, scale drawings, and other nonverbal items. Teachers in both reading and mathematics could benefit from suggestions by researchers in these areas.

7] Studies dealing with the effect of interest on textbook readability have been limited. Classroom teachers could benefit from such information when selecting content area reading materials.

References

Almy, Millie. *Young children's thinking.* New York: Teachers College Press, 1966.

Balow, I. H. Reading and computation ability as determinants of problem solving. *Arithmetic Teacher,* 1964, *11,* 18-22.

Brace, A., and Nelson, L. D. The pre-school child's concept of number. *Arithmetic Teacher,* 1966, *12,* 126-33.

Bruner, J. S. *The process of education.* Cambridge: Harvard University Press, 1960.

Bruner, J. S., Goodnow, Jacqueline J., and Austin, G. A. *A study of thinking.* New York: John Wiley and Sons, Inc., 1956.

Burns, P. C., and Yonally, J. L. Does the order of presentation of numerical data in multi-step arithmetic problems affect their difficulty? *School Science and Mathematics,* 1964, *64,* 267-70.

Cathcart, W. G., and Liedtke, W. Reflectiveness/impulsiveness and mathematics achievement. *Arithmetic Teacher,* 1969, *16,* 563-67.

Cawley, J. F., and Goodman, J. O. Interrelationships among mental abilities, reading, language arts, and arithmetic with the mentally retarded. *Arithmetic Teacher,* 1968, *15,* 631-36.

Chase, C. I. The position of certain variables in the prediction of problem solving. *Journal of Educational Research,* 1960, *54,* 9-14.

Chase, C. I. Formal analysis as a diagnostic technique in arithmetic. *Elementary School Journal,* 1961, *61,* 282-86.

Cleland, D. L., and Toussaint, Isabella H. The interrelationships of reading, listening, arithmetic computation, and intelligence. *Reading Teacher,* 1962, *15,* 228-31.

Corle, C. G., and Coulter, M. L. *The reading arithmetic skills program —a research project in reading and arithmetic.* University Park, Pennsylvania: The Pennsylvania School Study Council, 1964.

Faison, E. W. J. Readability of children's textbooks. *Journal of Educational Psychology,* 1951, *42,* 43-51.

Fay, L. Reading study skills: math and science. In J. A. Figurel (ed.), *Reading and Inquiry, Proceedings of the 10th Annual Convention of the International Reading Association,* 1965, *10,* 92-94.

Flavell, J. H. *The developmental psychology of Jean Piaget.* Princeton: D. Van Nostrand, 1963.

Glennon, V. J., and Callahan, L. G. *Elementary school mathematics; a guide to current research.* Washington: Association for supervision and curriculum development, 1968.

Heddens, J. W., and Smith, K. J. The readability of elementary mathematics textbooks. *Arithmetic Teacher*, 1964, *11*, 466-68.

Irish, Elizabeth H. Improving problem solving by improving verbal generalizations. *Arithmetic Teacher*, 1964, *11*, 169-75.

Johnson, D. A. The readability of mathematics books. *Mathematics Teacher*, 1957, *50*, 105-10.

Johnson, Mary E. The vocabulary difficulty of content subjects in grade five. *Elementary English*, 1952, *29*, 277-80.

Kerfoot, J. F. The vocabulary of primary arithmetic texts. *Reading Teacher*, 1961, *14*, 177-80.

Kline, M. Intellectuals and the schools: a case history. *Harvard Educational Review*, 1966, *36*, 505-11.

Kolson, C. The oral arithmetic vocabulary of kindergarten children. *Arithmetic Teacher*, 1963, *10*, 81-83.

Lyda, W. J., and Duncan, F. M. Quantitative vocabulary and problem solving. *Arithmetic Teacher*, 1967, *14*, 289-91.

Murray, F. B. Conservation of illusion distorted lengths and areas by primary school children. *Journal of Educational Psychology*, 1965, *59*, 62-66.

Murray, F. B. Cognitive conflict and reversibility training in the acquisition of length conservation. *Journal of Educational Psychology*, 1968, *59*, 82-87.

Piaget, J. How children form mathematical concepts. *Scientific American*, 1953, *189*, 74-79.

Piaget, J. *The child's concept of number.* New York: W. W. Norton and Company, 1965.

Piaget, J. Piaget's theory. Trans. by Guy Gellerier and Jonas Langer. In Paul Mussen (Ed.) *Carmichael's Manual of Child Psychology.* Vol. 1. New York: Wiley, 1970. Pp. 703-33.

Reed, Mary K. S. Vocabulary load of certain state-adopted mathematics textbooks, grades one through three. Unpublished doctoral dissertation, University of Southern California, 1965.

Repp, Florence. The vocabularies of five recent third grade arithmetic textbooks. *Arithmetic Teacher*, 1960, *7*, 128-32.

Reys, R. E., and Knowles, Lois. What is the status of elementary school textbooks? *Elementary School Journal*, 1968, *68*, 167-71.

Ross, R. A description of twenty underachievers. *Arithmetic Teacher*, 1964, *11*, 235-41.

Stern, Carolyn. Acquisition of problem-solving strategies in young children and its relation to verbalization. *Journal of Educational Psychology*, 1967, *58*, 245-52.

Stern, Carolyn, and Keislar, E. R. Acquisition of problem-solving strategies by young children and its relation to mental age. *American Educational Research,* 1967, *4,* 1-12.

Stull, Lorren L. Auditory assistance of reading as a factor in intermediate grade pupils' interpretation of verbal problems. Unpublished doctoral dissertation, The Pennsylvania State University, 1964.

Vanderlinde, L. F. Does the study of quantitative vocabulary improve problem solving? *Elementary School Journal,* 1964, *65,* 143-52.

Williams, Mary H., and McCreight, R. W. Shall we move the question? *Arithmetic Teacher,* 1965, *12,* 418-21.

Wilson, J. W. The role of structure in verbal problem solving. *Arithmetic Teacher,* 1967, *14,* 486-93.

Additional references

Alexander, V. E. Seventh graders' ability to solve problems. *School Science and Mathematics,* 1960, *60,* 603-06.

Ashlock, R. B. A test of understandings for the primary grades. *Arithmetic Teacher,* 1968, *15,* 438-41.

Brockman, Sister Mary A., and Reeves, A. W. Relationship between transiency and test achievement. *Alberta Journal of Educational Research,* 1967, *13,* 319-30.

Brueckner, L. J., Merton, E. L., and Grossnickle, F. E. *Moving ahead in arithmetic, Book 3.* (Teacher's Edition) New York: Holt, Rinehart, and Winston, 1963.

Bruner, J. S. *Toward a theory of instruction.* Cambridge: Harvard University Press, 1966.

Carroll, Anne W. The effects of segregated and partially integrated school programs on self-concept and academic achievement of educable mental retardees. *Journal of Exceptional Children,* 1967, *34,* 93-99.

Chase, C. I. The position of certain variables in the prediction of problem solving in arithmetic. *Journal of Educational Research,* 1960, *54,* 9-14.

Dobbs, Virginia, and Neville, D. The effect of non-promotion on the achievement of groups matched from retained first graders and promoted second graders. *Journal of Educational Research,* 1967, *60,* 472-75.

Elkind, D. Giant in the nursery—Jean Piaget. *New York Times,* May 26, 1968, 1, 25.

Feldhusen, J. F., Thurston, J. R., and Benning, J. J. Classroom behavior, intelligence and achievement. *Journal of Experimental Education*, 1967, *36*, 82-87.

Harper, R. J. C. Reading and arithmetic reasonings: a partial correlation and multiple regression analysis. *Alberta Journal of Educational Research*, 1957, *3*, 82-86.

Johnson, D. A. The readability of mathematics books. *Mathematics Teacher*, 1957, *50*, 105-10.

Kagan, J. Impulsive and reflective children: significance of conceptual tempo. In J. D. Krumboltz (Ed.), *Learning and the Educational Process*. Chicago: Rand McNally, 1965.

Keedy, M. L., Jameson, R. E., and Johnson, Patricia L. *Exploring modern mathematics, Book 2*. (Teacher's Edition) New York: Holt, Rinehart, and Winston, 1963.

Kramer, D. P., and Fleming, Elyse S. Interparental differences of opinion and children's academic achievement. *Journal of Educational Research*, 1966, *60*, 136-38.

Lyda, W. J., and Church, R. S. Direct, practical arithmetical experiences and success in solving realistic verbal reasoning problems in arithmetic. *Journal of Educational Research*, 1964, *57*, 530-33.

Monroe, W. S. The derivation of reasoning tests in arithmetic. *School and Society*, 1918, *8*, 295-99.

Motto, J. J., and Wilkins, Gayle S. Educational achievement of institutionalized emotionally disturbed children. *Journal of Educational Research*, 1968, *61*, 218-21.

Piaget, J., et al. The child's conception of geometry. E. A. Lunzer (Trans.). London: Routledge and Kegan Paul, 1960.

Roberts, G. H. The failure strategies of third grade arithmetic pupils. *Arithmetic Teacher*, 1968, *15*, 442-46.

Rosenblum, P. C. Implications of psychological research. In *The Low Achiever in Mathematics*. Washington: U. S. Department of Health, Education, and Welfare, 1966, Bulletin 31.

Spitzer, H. E., et al. *Mathematics concepts, properties, and operations, Grade 7*. (Teacher's Edition) St. Louis: Webster Division, McGraw-Hill Book Company, 1968.

Wiegand, R. A. Pittsburgh looks at readability of textbooks. *Journal of Reading*, 1967, *11*, 201-04.

Yeager, J. L. Measures of learning rates for elementary school students in mathematics and reading under a program of individually prescribed instruction. Unpublished doctoral dissertation, University of Pittsburgh, 1966.

Myron L. Coulter

Reading in mathematics: Classroom implications

The twentieth century scholars who have concentrated their vigorous research efforts upon the problems of reading the English language have described a variety of phenomena which appear to be permanently entrenched in the education of the young. Prominent among these phenomena is the identification of reading as a complex perception-response activity which is related in one form or another to practically every aspect of the instruction of the learner. Once reading was established as a complex act, entire research careers were developed around studies of the skills, attitudes, and numerous developmental characteristics required of the successful reader. This extensive research and its implementation have led to substantive improvements in the techniques and materials of reading instruction at nearly all learning levels. But perhaps most significantly, the teaching and learning of reading has been clearly established as a discipline of its own for purposes of research, teacher education, and school curriculum.

The almost universal practice of treating the elementary school reading program as a separate subject area has its own important implications. It established at least parity, and often a higher priority for reading when compared with the other areas of the curriculum. There are distinct and obvious advantages to the teaching of reading as a discrete body of skills. There can also be the serious drawback of isolating reading instruction from arithmetic, science, the social studies, and even the remaining language arts. Possibly the most serious result of this compartmentalization has been a tendency to accept the notion that reading instruction is the exclusive domain of the elementary teacher for a period of forty-five to sixty minutes per day. There has been good cause for this notion to develop, for it is only in recent years that any concerted efforts have been mounted to teach reading beyond the elementary school level. Fortunately, increasing attention is being given to the practice of developing reading competence as an essential factor in the mastery of curriculum content at all levels.

There is little doubt that teachers have done a splendid job of developing the fundamental skills of reading which can be applied to most learning areas. Children's vocabularies continue to expand with each generation; word and comprehension skills are better taught and better applied; reading interests and interest in reading are ever increasing; and the availability and utilization of books constantly set new records. These signs of excellent progress have established the value of the reading program as a distinct curriculum area, and it would be difficult indeed to remove it as a subject and spread its content of skills and literature throughout the remainder of the curriculum. Yet, reading is not merely a corpus of skills and literature which is to be mastered for its own merits. If reading programs are to attain fully their stated objectives of providing flexible, practical skills and positive attitudes for the reading of a wide variety of written matter, then these reading skills and attitudes must be taught and applied in all areas of the curriculum which rely upon reading competence as a learning mode.

As reported in the previous paper, research has indicated that many of the requisites for success in the elementary school arithmetic program are identical to those required for success in learning to read. Acceptable achievement in arithmetic was shown to be closely related to the child's ability to read well generally, to develop good oral language and vocabulary, to formulate concepts, to listen well, and to note detail. Specific as well as general skills in reading can, and often do, make the difference in whether the child understands the statements of problems and the instruction in principles contained in the arithmetic textbook. At times the written materials of arithmetic are substantially more difficult to comprehend than the child's reading instruction materials, and even the generally "good reader" is often in need of special assistance.

Reading tasks in arithmetic

Since arithmetic is by definition the science of numbers and computations which are expressed in very precise terms, it follows that the perception of those expressions necessarily requires equal precision. If the only reading task of the elementary school student were to accurately perceive the complex system of quantitative symbols, the study of arithmetic would be a much less rigorous requirement for him. However, such is not the case. Elementary school arithmetic is considerably more than a number system to be manipulated. It is a system expressed by numerals and explained in a verbal language. Unfortunately, the language is often far less precise and sometimes far more complex than the quantitative system which the student is expected to master. Herein lies the challenge. The student is confronted with an unequivocal content—numbers, which is presented in an equivocal medium—words. These words and the concepts which they embody pose a distinct problem of interpretation for the student, particularly if he is not a good reader or if he is not "mathematically inclined." Long before he can deal independently with the verbal arithmetic materials provided by the school he must learn the basic skills of reading. Then he must learn to apply those skills to a body of content which demands the utmost in accuracy and reasoning.

Even though it may be argued successfully that reading skill is not the primary concern of the elementary school arithmetic program, the researches reported have rather substantially documented the importance of good reading to good arithmetic achievement. Numerous studies have cited problems of readability of materials, of word study, of verbal problem solving, and of verbal concept interpretation as factors which have a direct bearing upon success in arithmetic. The research findings have also effectively established the need for continued attention throughout the elementary school years to a broad spectrum of specific arithmetic-reading skills.

These skills can be directly related to at least four major classes of reading tasks which the arithmetic materials require and upon which the classroom teacher can base arithmetic-reading instruction.

Task group 1: Understanding symbols and specialized devices

Each field of content has its unique system of notation, expression, and instrumentation which is developed to efficiently convey its core of knowledge with a high degree of standardization. Geography makes use of maps, charts, and the globe to represent the land masses and water bodies of the earth. Accompanying these tools is a system of notation—the cartographer's symbols used to depict natural and man-made phenomena such as rivers, mountains, political boundaries, cities, time boundaries, roadways, air routes, and scales of distance. These symbols must be learned and read with accuracy in order to adequately assimilate and relate the information which they contain.

Students who expect to learn and apply the discipline of music must master an intricate system of symbols which represent the infinite combinations of sounds and tempos that make them music instead of unblended noises. One can readily recognize this system of symbols as highly abstract, requiring extremely accurate discrimination if the student is to become master.

Equally abstract is the system of notations and expressions in the elementary school arithmetic materials. However, since these symbols are used almost daily by the older elementary school students as well as by adults, they may easily be presumed well known to all and scarcely in need of any special attention during instruction above the early primary years. This may well be true for commonly used symbols such as addition, subtraction, multiplication signs, the radical sign for division, and the equation sign. Likewise, whole numbers do not require a great deal of special instruction since they are used daily. Yet, with each succeeding level of arithmetic content new signs and expressions are introduced which do call for considerable emphasis because of their importance to learning the new concepts which they represent. The same is true for the wide variety of devices and instruments which are used in the study of quantity, distance, weight, area, volume, and time.

Expressions of quantity

Fractions. Even though the rudiments of reading and manipulating fractions may be introduced as early as the first grade, children of six or seven years of age have dealt almost exclusively with whole numbers. They need a great deal of practice in reading and interpreting quantitative expressions such as 1/2, 2/4, 4/8, 8/16, and 16/32, not to mention the odd fractional values such as 2/3, 3/5, 4/7, 5/9 and so on. A first tendency is often to read ½ as one-two rather than the more difficult one-half, or ⅔ as two-threes rather than two-thirds. However, once the proper fractions are reasonably familiar, the next step is to introduce the improper fractions such as 9/8 which youngsters are told to read as nine-eighths or as a mixed number, one and one-eighth. Coupled with the difficulty which some children experience in merely reading fractional expressions is the often confusing computation of fraction problems which introduces another somewhat complex reading problem. For instance, when adding one fraction to another only the numerators are added, providing the denominators are identical. Otherwise, the fractions must be *reduced* to the lowest common denominator. On the other hand, if fractions are to be multiplied, both numerator and denominator are multiplied regardless of their values. Even more difficult for the youngster is the division of one fraction by another in which the divisor is *inverted* and the fractions then multiplied. The correct interpretation and computation of fractions requires not only ability to reason well but also quite precise perceptual skills. Many children profit from the use of manipulative materials such as jig-sawed squares, circles, and lengths of heavy paper or board, together with written and verbal reinforcement by the teacher in developing not only a concept but also a perceptual image of fractional values. Skill in reading fractions can be greatly enhanced through the following steps:

1] Teach the names and ordinal values of denominators, e.g., /3 = third, /4 = fourth, /5 = fifth.

2] Stress the fact that the numerator should be read first and that it should be read as a cardinal number, one, two, three, etc., with emphasis on the idea that the numerator indicates how many there are of the denominator;

3] Provide oral reading practice, e.g., ⅔ is two-thirds and it means two of three parts of the whole;

4] Provide written practice, e.g., the fraction ¾ can be verbally expressed as *three fourths;*

5] Provide graphic or pictorial reinforcement, e.g., the coloring of three of the five pieces of a pie or the marking of three of the four segments of a bar.

Decimals and per cents. It is only a simple process of division to convert a proper fraction into a decimal equivalent and hence to a per cent value, but there is a substantial gulf of reading and reasoning to be bridged before a youngster understands that ½ = .5 = .50 = 50% = 50¢. He must have a solid foundation in reading and understanding the differences between tens and tenths, hundreds and hundredths, etc., in numerical as well as verbal form before these expressions will make sense to him. Even though decimal fractions are introduced in the late elementary grades, a long-known medium such as monetary values, using $1.00 as the base, can be helpful to students who find decimals difficult to read and comprehend. Another valuable tool to strengthen the reading of decimal values is a table of decimal equivalents, which can be found in some arithmetic texts and certainly in an encyclopedia or engineering handbook. Such a table provides the reader with a comprehensive list of proper fractions and their decimal equivalents and provides plenty of practice in reading decimals in tenths, hundredths, and ten thousandths.

Numbers of greater magnitude. There may be more occasions for reading numbers of greater magnitude in nonarithmetic materials than in the arithmetic text, but this skill is quite properly taught in the arithmetic program. Most elementary school students readily learn to read numbers in tens and hundreds but may often falter when they encounter the thousands, hundred thousands, and millions. A number such as 1,075,011 may cause a youngster more difficulty than 1,750,110 because in the first number the hundred-thousand and hundred values are missing. In such cases it may be helpful for him to read the number from the right-to-left because he probably has learned units, tens, hundreds, thousands, ten thousands, hundred thousands, and millions in that order. Therefore, he would read 11, 75 thousand, one million which should then be reversed, without inserting the word *and* for the commas. It is quite likely that elementary school students will have many more occasions to read and write large numbers in numeric form than in verbal terms. However, practice in reading these higher order numbers can be augmented by having the students write them in words. In order to be accurately written in verbal terms, the number must first be read correctly. Thus, the first example would be written: one million, seventy-five thousand, eleven.

Proper fractions are equivalent to, but not written in the same form as, decimal fractions; and tens and hundreds are related to, but of vastly different value than, tenths and hundredths. Therefore, each of these expressions requires perceptual skill, and unless the student can exercise acute discrimination among these symbols he will experience frustration and lack of readiness for the subsequent requirements of mathematics.

Expressions and instruments of linear measurement

Most of the gross measures of length and distance will be familiar to even the beginning elementary school student. He will know something of the inch, the foot, the yard, and the mile and can readily learn to read the inch marks labeled on the one-foot rule or the yardstick, and the miles and tenths of miles indicated on an odometer. Beyond this extent practically every youngster will need considerable help and practice in reading the fractional divisions of the 1/8-inch, 1/16-inch, or 1/32-inch scaled rule. The concept of scale and the reading of scaled distance have at least two important applications to the student. He will doubtlessly deal with scaled drawings of materials, construction plans, and land areas in the arithmetic program. And he will surely be expected to read scaled distances (such as the $\frac{1}{63,360}$, or one-inch-equal-one-mile scale) in the social studies. These reading skills can be taught with high success once a firm understanding of fractions is established. In fact, the use of a simple scale such as $1'' = 1'$; $\frac{1}{2}'' = 1'$ can be helpful in providing practice in the study of fractions.

As the student reaches the upper elementary grades, he will come into contact with the metric system of linear measure, which will require considerable study of the terms *millimeter, centimeter, meter,* and *kilometer,* as well as comparative use of the meter stick and the yardstick. As a system of linear measurement, the metric scale has far less frequent application in our society than the standard English system, yet there are enough uses of the metric system to establish it as quite deserving of attention in the instructional program. Those students who develop interests in various fields of science will find their knowledge of the metric system of measurements invaluable. If for no other reason, the introduction of the symbols, terms, and devices of the system during the elementary grades will prove a distinct advantage to the students who will study mathematics and other sciences.

Reading expressions of area and volume

Area. Up to this time the student's thinking has dealt primarily with one-dimensional values such as the whole number, a fraction of that number, the arithmetical manipulation of the number, and length, distance, or time. The interpretation of area will now require the student to think of and read expressions in two dimensions. He must visualize a length and a width of space which he is either reading from a drawing or attempting to draw. Not only must he think in two dimensions but also he will most often find area expressed in scaled proportions rather than in full size. For instance, a square foot or a square mile can hardly be shown full-size in his text or workbook, so he will read them as scaled representations of the actual areas.

If area were expressed only as the combination of the length and width of a regular two-dimensional geometric shape such as a rectangle or a square, the reading of this quantity could be rather easily developed. However, since an area can assume any shape described by an enclosing line or lines, and since it can be expressed in several terms such as square feet or square miles, the student is faced with the problem of reading a geometric figure whose sides may have varying values and whose mass may be expressed in one of a variety of verbal terms.

The elementary school arithmetic program rarely goes beyond the study of areas which can be described by either a square or oblong rectangle. Therefore, the reading of the dimensions of an area is somewhat simplified when compared to the advanced study of areas described by circles or polygons and is based primarily upon the multiplication of length by width. It is important to create several understandings, however. One is the identification of two dimensions. Another is that area may be expressed in several terms such as square feet or acres. A third is that area does not imply only a square or rectangular shape. And a fourth is a clear distinction of the differences between area and perimeter.

Volume. For the purposes of the elementary school student, the understanding of volume is closely related to his knowledge of area and, of course, is distinguished by the consideration of three dimensions rather than two. In most of the elementary arithmetic materials, volume is expressed as the amount which a container will hold, and it is calculated by the three dimensional formula of length multiplied by width, multiplied by height. If the upper elementary student has a good understanding of area and its derivation, he should experience little difficulty in grasping the meaning of volume, although the teacher must be sure that the concept is clear and distinct. The use of three-dimensional objects such as boxes should be equally as helpful in establishing the concept of volume as would be the use of two-dimensional figures in developing the meaning of area.

The skill of reading to note detail is most closely related to the tasks of reading the expressions of linear measurement, area, and volume. The teacher may both teach and test this skill through several approaches.

1] Require students to look briefly at an expression such as a dimension or a scale of distance and then write the expression and describe its meaning; for instance 50' x 20', the base and height of a rectangle; $1'' = 1'$, the 1/12 scale; 4' x 3' x 2', the length, width, and height of an object which describes its volume.

2] Provide practice in identifying the correct symbolic expression for a verbal cue; for example, "What scale is represented by a two-inch line which equals two linear feet?" ($2'' = 1'$, $2' = 1'$, $\underline{1'' = 1'}$, $1'' = 2'$)

3] Provide practice in rapid location in the textbook of symbols for verbal or written expressions given by the teacher; for example, "Write the dimensions given in this chapter for: an area of 36 square feet (6' x 6'); a volume of 36 cubic feet (3' x 3' x 4'); a perimeter of 36 feet (8' x 10' x 9' x 9')."

4] Check accuracy of immediate recall of details just read; for example, "What was the fractional expression of the scale which is used in the set of line drawings?" (1/12 or 1 to 12)

Reading expressions and devices of time

Assuming that every child in the first two or three years of school will receive detailed instruction in reading the hours, minutes, and seconds of a clock; the days and years of the calendar; and the numeration system of the years and decades of a century, he should have the foundation for reading at least two devices of time which he will probably encounter in grade five or six. Traditionally one of the more tedious-to-read instruments of time is the schedule of operations issued by the various airline, bus, and railroad companies. There is a wide variation in format, different systems of symbols, and sometimes very complicated routings, all of which may cause the user to logically resort to the telephone for expert assistance from a reservations clerk. In the event that a timetable, but no telephone, is available there are some tips that a reader should bear in mind when figuring his own schedule. First he should look for effective dates of the schedule, the time zone used, and the notation of any special features such as heavier type for afternoon and evening hours. After locating the desired routing, the reader should carefully determine whether the train, bus, or plane is operating on the weekday, weekend, or holiday during which he plans to travel and what type of equipment is being used. He may also wish to check the number of stops en route in order to satisfy his preference of lapsed travel time. Once he has mapped out his schedule, he should make reservations with the company agent who will give him all the information he has just laboriously put together. But it is a good idea to know how to read a timetable, anyhow, if for no other reason than the fact that these types of exercises still appear in many arithmetic texts and work materials of the upper elementary school.

Another method of relating time and events is the time line, a figure which resembles a scaled continuum of significant occurrences and the dates on which they took place. The time line may be thematic and show the dates of all or only the most important events of a similar type, such as the earthquakes on the Pacific Coast from 1900 to 1971. Or the time line may be chronological and catalog all or only the most important national events of a specific period such as one year, regardless of the nature of the event. It is one of the best means of highlighting periods of peak activity over a long stretch of time, such as the record of severe weather phenomena in a particular region over the past 50 years. These graphic devices may also be effective for illustrating a predicted schedule of major events, for instance, the next 100 years of space exploration. The time line has many effective uses and can be a valuable aid to the reader or writer who wishes to visualize a series of meaningful dates in relation to one another.

Reading systems of weights and measures

Possibly the best assistance the teacher can give the student in reading weights is to provide ample opportunity for guided reference work in tables of weights and measures. Students should receive instruction in determining the basic differences in the several standards of weights such as the English and American (avoirdupois) system (16 ounces to the pound), the metric system of grams, and the Troy Weight system (12 ounces to the pound). Of course, the avoirdupois system is the most widely used in England and the United States, but familiarity with other systems will be advantageous to the student as he reads and works with science and social studies materials in addition to arithmetic.

The values of liquid and dry measures are often regarded as closely related to the measures of weight, very probably because they are presented in table form along with the weight measures at the end of most arithmetic texts and also because the various measurement systems are often treated as one unit of instruction. As in the case of reading weights, these systems can be effectively taught with reference exercises requiring the use of tables. And, whenever practical, instruments such as the balance and standard-sized containers such as pints, quarts, and pecks are very helpful in reinforcing the concept and reading skills necessary for utilizing the measurement systems.

The examples of the wide variety of symbols, language, and

devices in this task group are meant to illustrate the peculiar reading demands which the discipline imposes upon the student. The suggestions for improving reading skills are by no means exhaustive, but rather are offered as examples of the many techniques the arithmetic teacher can use to assist his students in reading with precision.

Task group 2: Understanding the general organization of the material

To this point the discussion has attempted to establish that good general reading skills and the ability to interpret accurately the unique systems of notation are essential to the effective study of fields of content. Needless to say, these skills are important only if they are applied to some verbal medium, such as the printed page. And every academic area of the elementary school program places heavy emphasis upon printed material, which in turn places an equal burden upon the student to cope with a variety of content in the curriculum.

The instructional materials of the several subject areas differ not only in content, but also in style, structure, and format. For example, a history text which is often organized into chapters or divisions of chronological events and written in narrative style presents a format quite dissimilar to that of a language or spelling book with its topical organization and exercise-oriented layout. Likewise, a science text with its somewhat technical treatment of a wide range of scientific topics and its emphasis on methodology in experimentation and discovery of natural phenomena represents a substantially different content organization from that of a general reading textbook which contains a wide variety of literary styles and broad theme parcels of prose and poetry supplemented with highly specialized study exercises in reading skills and appreciation.

The arithmetic text departs from all others in format and style, with primary concern placed upon the logical sequence of arithmetic skills and principles, less emphasis upon theme organization and literary style, and the use of non-story-type written exercises to illustrate or provide practice in mathematical concepts and rules. Although the arithmetic study materials rightfully stress quantitative concepts rather than literary and reading skills, the materials remain to be read. The student who is aware of the organization and peculiar characteristics of the material he is expected to study will approach the text or workbook with much greater confidence and readiness.

The student's acquaintance with his study materials quite obviously begins when the teacher introduces the materials at the outset of an instructional period. The manner in which the texts or workbooks are presented can make a difference in the student's grasp of their contents and purposes. If the use of the materials begins by proceeding directly to the first page of the first chapter and continues in the same manner, most children will probably follow the directions rather well and complete the daily assignments, but few will understand how one section of the text is related to another or what they are ultimately working toward. If, on the other hand, a reasonable amount of time is spent in orienting the student to his new book, he should be much better prepared to use the book in the manner which the author and teacher intend. The teacher could employ some or all of the suggestions below depending upon the maturity of the students and the complexity of the material.

General description of the text

Give a brief sketch of the author's background. Students frequently do not know or care about the author as they should. In many cases, the students may have genuine questions about a fact or statement made by an author, and they should be encouraged to go to the extent of writing him for an explanation. Most authors are pleased to have this contact with school children, and the students may develop more interest in critical reading if it can result in correspondence with an author.

Overview of the organization of content

Arithmetic texts are not all organized alike. Some have chapters, some have topical units, and others do not appear to have discrete divisions of content, but instead may present the content much as a continuum of concepts with only a new heading to introduce the next concept. It may be helpful to compare or contrast the text to be used with other arithmetic texts or with those of subjects such as science and social studies in order to illustrate the distinctive organization of the text to be studied.

The scope of the material

An examination of the table of contents not only will provide the range and depth of the content included but also it will provide an understanding of the sequence of treatment. If the teacher plans any substantive deviations from the scope and sequence outlined in the table of contents, this would be an appropriate time to discuss it with the students. This phase of the introduction of materials also can be helpful to the teacher in determining whether the students have been given any background for the early parts of the content during their previous instructional levels. At times the teacher can spot particular strengths and weaknesses in a student's background or general areas of content which must be reviewed before the next level of difficulty is introduced.

Distinctive characteristics of the content

Quite often the style of written matter in an arithmetic text varies from that of other subject area books. It is helpful to the student if the teacher points out that the verbal problems are written for a different purpose than those of most other text materials, that they emphasize quantitative concepts, key procedural words, and computation process. For these reasons the verbal problems must be read very carefully.

Attention should also be called to the importance of accuracy in reading numerical expressions, to graphic illustrations of various types, and to the manner in which arithmetic principles and rules are presented. The text generally follows a similar pattern of lesson study throughout. This pattern should be carefully described so that the students will spend their time on the more important matter of discovering mathematical facts and not in trying to discover the routine of a lesson. If the teacher has any particular preferences for a different study pattern, they should be thoroughly discussed and understood by the students at this time. The teacher should give the students all the help he can for making the study of the text as clearly understood as possible.

Special features of the text

A textbook generally provides a great deal of help to the student. There should be an examination with brief practical examples of helpful study aids such as the index, reference information, tables of weights and measures, the glossary of terms, footnotes, and decimal equivalents. The more thoroughly the student understands such features, the more apt he will be to use them as routine aids to arithmetic mastery. Furthermore, these types of references should be used in virtually every academic activity, and even students who are classed as good to excellent readers can profit much from extensive work with indices, tables, and other referencing materials.

If tests are to be administered or taken independently as they occur in the text, it would be advisable to discuss their purposes and the uses made of the results. For instance, some tests may be given prior to a period of instruction for diagnostic purposes. Others may be administered subsequent to instruction or study in order to assess achievement in that particular body of knowledge or skill. At best, tests represent a mild threat to most students, and if the teacher will discuss their uses, there will be better understanding if not relief.

A good understanding of the general format and special features of any instructional materials will prove helpful not only to the students but to the teacher as well. Familiarity with organization and content constitutes one of the major reasons why many teachers are understandably reluctant to change from a long-used text to a new one, even though the new material may prove superior to the old. If the teacher is to remain the master of the instructional program he must be thoroughly knowledgeable of the materials to the extent that he can adapt freely to his students' needs when they are not accommodated by the study materials. Otherwise, the materials dominate the program and determine not only the parameters of content but the teaching strategy as well.

Task group 3: Developing the arithmetic vocabulary

As discussed above, the readability of an arithmetic text is affected by several factors such as the general format, the uses of illustration, and the special features which are designed to aid the reader. But probably the greatest influences upon the reading ease or difficulty of the verbal material are exerted by the vocabulary and concept burden and the length of sentences. In fact, the proportion of hard words and the average length of sentences are two of the principal factors in several widely used formulas which are employed to determine an approximation of the grade-level difficulty of reading matter.

The application of these readability formulas can indeed yield a percentage of words in a passage or book which do not appear on the lengthy list of familiar words that accompanies the formulas. However, this information does not reveal the particular concepts embodied in many of the hard words nor the reader's understanding of either the word or the concept. Because of these difficulties, the older readability formulas are gradually giving way to the more recently developed cloze technique which offers the reader a chance to supply missing strategic terms within context material, thereby providing a measure of his understanding of both vocabulary and concept, as well as context. This approach of basing the difficulty level of written materials upon the reader's ability to handle it is gaining favor with researchers, teachers, and authors. Because it provides for a previously missing dimension—the interaction of the reader and his vocabulary with contextual materials, the cloze technique is very likely a much more realistic measure of the reading difficulty of materials. Even though this is not the place to establish the validity of the cloze procedure, an example of the importance of concept knowledge rather than mere acquaintance with a sizeable stock of words seems appropriate. For instance, it would be very difficult to find many fifth-grade students who do not know the words *great* and *circle*. It would probably be far less difficult, however, to find a large number of fifth graders who know the words but who do not understand the *great circle* concept of aerial navigation. There can be a substantial gulf between word recognition and word power.

Assuming, therefore, that the student with a well-developed stock of vocabulary terms and concepts will have the advantage over his peer who does not possess these virtues, it would seem quite reasonable for the arithmetic teacher to do what he can to improve the verbal facilities of all his students. *Vocabulary* and *concept* are closely related terms. A reading vocabulary is that fund of terms which one recognizes in print. The concept is a mental set or idea for the vocabulary term; it is frequently triggered by the recognition of the verbal term. Therefore, the context in which the word is encountered has considerable bearing upon the concept which the reader will evoke. As an example, the word *products* will suggest one concept in a social studies context and quite another if the student is reading about the processes of multiplication.

There are large numbers of words which have widely varied applications in the several fields of content. A word such as *state* which is used differently with reference to 1] liquids, solids, and gases in science; 2] a geographic area in the social studies; and 3] a verb meaning "to assert" in the language arts, may cause some students as much if not more difficulty than highly technical terms with discrete meanings. The fact that a student may know a word with multiple meanings in one context is no assurance that he will know the word in other contexts.

The interchangeable vocabulary

There are numerous words and expressions that have one meaning in arithmetic materials and quite different meanings in other materials. These very commonly used terms can often cause confusion to a reader, particularly if he is the type of person who learns one definition or use of a word and is satisfied that he knows the word. These interchangeable terms are often so well known (at least by one general definition) that little attention is given them, even when they appear with a new meaning or in a different context. And yet, if three or four persons are asked to write one meaning of the same word, such as *race,* it often develops that there are as many definitions as there are writers.

Meanings of words are quite often related to the individual's background, and, therefore, a teacher should not assume that all students will have the same definition or concept of the same arithmetic term. Below is a listing of several terms which commonly appear in arithmetic materials. Each of the words has at least two significant meanings, and some have as many as 15 to 17 different uses. If one thinks of these terms in an arithmetic context, the chances are that only one definition or use will come to mind immediately. However, with an instant's reflection, several uses of each term become readily apparent, and in fact, the nonarithmetic uses of some of the words may seem more frequent or more important than the way the word is used in an arithmetic context.

The terms:

area	mean	root
cardinal	median	round
difference	partition	set
dimension	product	solution
dividend	proper	table
foot	radical	scale
improper	reduce	yard

These, of course, are but a few of the dozens of common interchangeable terms which may occur in content fields other than arithmetic. But, the fact that they are common should by no means imply that they do not need attention. On the contrary, the teacher should be particularly watchful for these interchangeable terms and make certain that the students understand the specific use for each one in its arithmetic context. These vocabulary items should be identified in advance of the time the students encounter them in the text, and they should be presented as part of the routine arithmetic vocabulary instruction each week.

A few additional suggestions for teaching terms such as the above may be helpful.

1] List two or more meanings for each term and ask students to identify the proper meaning for use in arithmetic; for example, *dividend*: an additional payment; a number to be divided.

2] Ask students to illustrate the arithmetic meaning of the vocabulary terms with appropriate mathematical symbols, expressions, or objects; for example, *reduce* $= (4/8 = \frac{1}{2})$, *round* $= (\$4.75$ becomes $\$5.00)$, *yard* $= (3$ feet$)$.

3] Introduce new areas of study in arithmetic with a study of the terms the students will use. A short, snappy, periodic vocabulary review may help many students, especially those who are not the best readers.

4] Test for vocabulary power as well as ability in reasoning and computation.

The technical vocabulary

The vocabulary of interchangeable items represents only one portion of the word study program in arithmetic. This discipline, as all others, has its body of rather technical terms which are unique to arithmetic or mathematics. This does not mean that such terms would be found only in an arithmetic textbook, but it does mean that regardless of its location it will always have an arithmetic or mathematic meaning.

There are obviously hundreds of technical terms within the total scope of the field of mathematics. These specialized words and expressions are far too numerous to list; therefore, only a few of the items which are representative of those found in the elementary school arithmetic materials are included here. The terms:

add	fraction	partial product
angle	higher decade	per cent
circle	lowest term	perimeter
computation	minuend	quotient
cube root	mixed number	ratio
decimal	multiplicand	rectangle
denominator	multiply	subtract
divide	numerator	subtrahend
divisor	ordinal	triangle

In most cases, if any vocabulary study is conducted, it will be with the technical terms such as those above. An understanding of the unique terminology of arithmetic is essential to mastery; therefore, study and review of the special vocabulary are required on an almost daily basis. A few suggestions may prove helpful in teaching the arithmetic vocabulary.

1] Make very few assumptions that the students are familiar with all terms. Words such as *divisor, place value, partial product, annexing, reducing, balance,* and *compound* will be quite well known to the teacher, but perhaps less familiar to many students. The glossaries and indices of textbooks and teachers' manuals are good sources of terms which can be quickly tried with students for understanding. Each new area of study in the arithmetic program should include a study of the terminology of that content.

2] Be sure that all words are correctly pronounced and spelled. This suggestion applies to any use of the language. However, the elementary school arithmetic program often requires less oral reading and written work than other curriculum areas, and the teacher may be less well informed of the youngsters' precise usage of arithmetic terms. Mispronunciation and misspelling are often root causes of misunderstanding, particularly in verbal problem study. Language accuracy should be given the same degree of importance as computational accuracy.

3] Assist students in applying word attack skills to unfamiliar terms. Students will thus become aware that word attack techniques such as phonic and structural analysis have practical applications in subject areas as well as in the reading instruction program.

4] When a specialized term is called for, use it. Avoid substituting less precise terms. For example, if a process calls for *ordinal position,* this term should be used rather than *place in line* or some similar substitute. Obviously, when a new term is introduced it is often necessary to describe its meaning with more familiar, but less precise, words. After the introduction, the new term should be used whenever appropriate, without substitution. Laxity in the use of accurate terminology has been the major contributing factor to meaningless general expressions such as *things* and *stuff* in the speech patterns of many people. The field of arithmetic can ill afford the use of "easy" substitutes for precision.

5] Provide opportunities for using new terms in a variety of ways—reading, speaking, writing, drawing, etc.— to reinforce understanding. The broader and the more frequent the student's application of newly acquired terminology, the sooner and the more naturally he will use his expanded vocabulary.

6] In testing, check for growth in vocabulary as well as in reasoning and computation. Specific items which test the knowledge of technical and common arithmetic terms should become as routine as the testing of problem-solving skills. Students should be expected to write definitions, match the term with its arithmetic application, and supply the accurate term for a described function. Arithmetic vocabulary testing can be of substantive assistance in diagnosing a student's growth in understanding of the subject.

The arithmetic vocabulary is the backbone of the textbook, since it is the medium by which the concepts and processes are conveyed to the student. This vocabulary, consisting of both unique and interchangeable terms, must meet one criterion above all others. It must be precise, for without precision arithmetic is no longer a science.

The requirement of language precision pertains not only to the writer and teacher, but to the student as well. The language must be read just as accurately as it is written. Each arithmetic program, from kindergarten through the highest levels, should regularly devote a segment of the instructional time to a systematic study of the words, concepts, and symbols found in the materials. Knowledge of the vocabulary directly affects the student's arithmetic reasoning and is every ounce as important as the mastery of computational processes.

Task group 4: Reading to solve verbal problems

The elementary school student is introduced to verbal problems as early as first grade. Once the basic number concepts and the simple arithmetic functions have been presented, it is quite common that the first form of written problems—following of simple written directions—will appear. At first the teacher will provide a great deal of assistance by reading the statements to the class or child and by showing examples. This is rather important, since there may be some youngsters who understand number concepts and functions but who have not progressed well enough in their reading skills to understand the written directions.

From the simple direction-following problems the materials may proceed quite rapidly to the two- and three-sentence verbal problems which provide quantitative information in the first and second sentences and then ask the student to find a particular solution in the last sentence. This type of problem often appears as a summary exercise which follows a number of pages of computation and is used to determine the student's ability to solve a practical problem after a new function or concept has been presented. The construction of the problem statements in these exercises tends to be quite uniform and the content of all problem statements closely related to the concept or principle to be learned. Due to this uniformity, the primary-grade student can easily read the remaining problems in a set after the first one has been completed.

However, as the level of difficulty of the arithmetic increases, it is accompanied by an increase in verbal problem reading difficulty. For, even though these problems are designed primarily to provide practice in arithmetic reasoning, in selecting the proper solution procedures, and in relating arithmetic to everyday life, they do require an ever-widening range of comprehension skills.

The reader of the intermediate-grade materials will have to be alert to key descriptive words, e.g., *average-annual, rate, maximum, minimum, share,* and *share equally,* which can make the difference in a correct solution. He must also identify certain procedural terms such as *difference, per,* and *combined,* which will help him select the proper solution process. The efficient reader will quickly locate and put aside irrelevant information in the problem statement and work with the essential facts only. At the same time he can quickly supply missing information needed for the problem solution, such as the number of quarts in a gallon, pounds in a ton, or feet in a mile. Above all, the elementary school student must first learn to interpret the problem statement literally, rather than inferentially, or he will probably tend to read arithmetic problems as poorly as some of them are written. For instance consider this problem:

George has a candy bar which is in three sections.
If he shares the candy with Jack, how many sections will Jack get?

The less careful reader, as the less careful problem writer, will probably incorrectly interpret the verb *shares* to mean *divides equally* and answer, "One and one-half sections." The good reader who interprets the statement literally will not excuse the clumsy writing and will correctly answer, "Jack will get as many sections as George wishes to give him." Of course this answer will not be accepted, but the good reader has a legitimate reason to ask the author of the problem what the word *shares* means to him.

The writer of arithmetic materials is not necessarily concerned with the readability level of the material for all students; he is primarily interested in teaching a quantitative concept through a verbal medium. Unfortunately, readability and the understanding of arithmetic processes are inseparably related in the verbal problem, and the writer who overburdens the written problem with heavy vocabulary, complicated statements, and imprecise language usually creates a difficult situation for both the poor and the able reader. For instance, a difficult vocabulary will bother the less able reader more than the good reader; a complex problem statement will be difficult for the slower reader, but an imprecise statement may cause the good critical reader more trouble than it does the poorer reader. As an example of the imprecise statement, consider the following verbal problem which resembles one that appeared in a widely used arithmetic textbook:

> Jane has 50 tomato plants. If she plants them in four rows how many will there be in each row? Will there be any plants left over?

This problem was written to reinforce understanding of division of whole numbers with a remainder. Therefore, any reader would know that he should have a remainder since the entire lesson deals with remainders. However, a critical reader would immediately answer that there would be no remainder, since the statement says Jane plants them (all 50) in four rows. If she plants them, there will not be any left over. Yet, the teacher's answer sheet showed a remainder of two in the correct solution. The good reader will also penalize himself if he does not assume that Jane planted an *equal number* of tomato plants in each of the four rows, although there is no good reason to believe that all rows had an equal number of plants. Therefore, the answer to the question of how many will be in each row can be "one or more." The writer probably intended that the problem read:

> Jane has 50 tomato plants. If she plants an equal number of them in each of four rows, how many plants will there be in each row? How many will be left over, if any?

The student now must divide 50 by four and should arrive at correct solution of 12 plants in each row, with two plants left over.

The good reader can also be penalized if he literally interprets the following problem:

> How many gallons of maple syrup will fill 32 quart cans?

The correct answer, of course, is "any number of eight or above." Eight gallons will fill 32 quart cans as will 20 gallons or 100 gallons. A student would be literally correct if he would give any number above eight, but his answer would quite likely be scored as incorrect, because the writer wanted to know *exactly* how many gallons, even though he did not so state the problem.

The point of these illustrations is that the materials sometimes place unfair demands upon the reader, and often the good reader is the one who must forgive the writer and work out the problem in the way that he thinks the writer intended. If verbal problems are to require precision in reading (which they should), then they must be phrased in a manner that will reward, not penalize, accurate interpretation.

Specific suggestions for emphasis

In addition to the suggestions given in the examples above there are a few recommendations which may prove quite helpful in improving students' skills in reading verbal problems.

1] Select a number of verbal problems which require different reading skills and write a series of questions about each problem, rather than simply call for quantitative solutions.

> Example: Identifying descriptive words
> Each spring the school held a marble shooting contest, with prizes for the winners. One of the rules for entering the contest

was that each person must have a minimum of 50 marbles. Jack, Harry, and Bill were three friends who wanted to enter. Jack had 75 marbles, Harry had 50 marbles, but Bill had only 40 marbles. The boys realized that one of them could not enter the contest. They decided to combine their marbles and share them equally to see if they would each have enough marbles to become contestants.

What does the word *combine* mean in this problem?

What does the word *minimum* mean in this problem?

Could a person enter the contest if he had more than 50 marbles?

Could a person enter the contest if he had fewer than 50 marbles?

After combining their marbles, what was the total number the boys had?

How many marbles did each boy have after they shared the marbles?

Which boy lost the most marbles by sharing them?

Which boy gained the most marbles by sharing them?

Could all three boys enter the contest?

Do you think these boys were good friends? Why or why not?

(Corle and Coulter, 1962)

2] Select or write a few problems which are worded so that they are insoluble and ask the students to identify the weaknesses.

Example:

Mrs. Smith earned $20 for each full day she worked in a bakery. How many weeks would she have to work to earn $600?

3] Have students rewrite poorly worded problems and write accurate, original problems for classmates to solve.

4] Test the students' abilities to read problems critically by using the above procedure.

The use of questions related to each problem has been shown to be effective in helping youngsters think through problems prior to attempting an arithmetic solution. Students with the basic word attack and literal comprehension skills appropriate to their developmental levels should have little difficulty improving their abilities to interpret arithmetic problems accurately.

Conclusions

The classroom practices for improving the reading of arithmetic materials were arranged in four task groups related to 1] general readability as affected by language, symbols, and specialized devices, 2] the organization of the instructional materials, 3] the development of the arithmetic vocabulary, and 4] the reading and interpretation of verbal problems. A summary of the more important influences upon arithmetic readability may serve as a guideline for the teacher who is interested in assisting his students to improve their arithmetic reading skills.

1] The language of the elementary school arithmetic materials may present a greater challenge to many students than the quantitative expressions, concepts, and operations which are to be mastered. This language difficulty may be related to one or more of several factors which can cause some problems for even the good readers. First, the language usually serves as a medium to convey mathematical concepts and functions and seldom is written in the style or format of the familiar narrative found in general reading materials. This is a quite proper but a quite different use of the language. Next, due to the nature of the content there is generally less concern by the author for vocabulary control, and the material is often more heavily burdened with concept and vocabulary than are the less technical materials at the same instructional level. Another factor which affects readability is the improperly written verbal problem. Many poorly phrased problem statements have been written into widely used materials with the unfortunate result that students are forced to either ignore the imprecision or "fill in" the unintentionally missing language. Critical reading ability can be a handicap in this instance.

2] One of the more important reading tasks that is easily overlooked in any content field instruction is that of understanding the general and specific organization of the teaching-learning materials and the requirements for study which these materials pose to the student. The materials of the various fields of study differ widely, and the student who is aware of the

organization and scope of the content, the distinctive characteristics of the content as compared with other fields, and the special features of the text he is using will have a real advantage
which would otherwise not be true.

3] In addition to the learning of thousands of combinations
of symbols known as the alphabet, the reader's problems are
further complicated by a new level of symbolic notation which is
introduced with the system of numerals and the unique symbols
of arithmetic. The student must cope with these abstractions,
and he must reason verbally as well as quantitatively in order to
be a successful achiever. In order to relieve the reader as he is
learning the new system of symbols, the teacher should deal
with the tangible, the concrete, the manipulative means of introducing new concepts whenever practical. He should build upon
the known, teach through the most objective means available,
and proceed to the more abstract levels as the student's progress
allows.

4] The learning materials of arithmetic, as do those of
other content fields, contain a vocabulary of unique technical
terms and a large stock of terms which are interchangeable with
one or more other fields of content. In most instances, the technical vocabulary tends to receive the greatest instructional emphasis, since that vocabulary is essential to the intelligent utilization of the materials. The more generalized vocabulary, consisting of usually well-known words or expressions from other
contexts, may be overlooked because of an unfortunate assumption that a word or concept that is familiar in one context is familiar in all contexts. An example of such an interchangeable
term is the word *round* which has a meaning in music that is
substantially different from its meaning in arithmetic. The general as well as the technical vocabulary requires emphasis. A
highly developed vocabulary will not assure the student of mastery of arithmetic content, but a poorly developed vocabulary
will almost certainly hold promise of failure.

5] If the traditional arithmetic textbook has any identifiable
short-coming, it may well be the inconsistencies in the language
of written problems. Far too often the authors of texts have

forced both good and poor readers to make precarious assumptions about a problem statement. This is due to the imprecise wording of the problem in which key terms such as *exactly, equally, each,* and *equal share* are only implied and represent a trap for the critical reader who interprets the statement literally.

Good reading ability demands accuracy. This requirement should not be sacrificed for the sake of the written problem. The problem statement must stand the test of accuracy of expression, and the accurate reader should be rewarded, not penalized, for his correct interpretations.

6] Students who have been taught to analyze the structure of a verbal problem statement will encounter far less difficulty in deciding upon solution processes. The teacher who helps the student to read the problem statement accurately to look for the relevant clues and to formulate a solution process consistent with the facts presented will have made a worthy contribution to the student's repertoire of skills in the fields of arithmetic.

There are a few suggestions for the improvement of readability which may be of interest to the writers who prepare arithmetic teaching materials and to the teachers who select and use them.

1] There should be numerous exercises throughout the materials designed to improve the reading skills which are required. The exercise should be related to the various reading tasks described in this paper.

2] Further attention should be given to relating the vocabulary of the materials to at least the general reading level of students for whom the materials are written. The use of cloze procedures and readability formulas can assist in assessing the concept burden and vocabulary level. Obviously, easier and less precise terms cannot substitute for any required technical terminology.

3] Perhaps most important, there should be quite accurate language utilization in all verbal problem state-

ments.   Inaccurately worded statements are significant contributors to incorrect solutions by students.
Too often a literal interpretation of the language will
lead the good reader to a solution which the author
did not intend, and the student is therefore penalized
for reading too well.

References

Corle, C. G., and Coulter, M. L. Lesson V, Vocabulary and Word Usage—Descriptive Words. *Reading-Arithmetic Skills Program, Workbook in Problem Reading for Grades 4, 5, and 6.* University Park, Pennsylvania: The Pennsylvania School Study Council, 1962. Pp. 11-12.

George G. Mallinson

Reading in the sciences:
A review of the research

The statement by James Allen, former United States Commissioner of Education affirming every child's "right to read" is difficult to challenge. However, one wonders why, in 1970, such a statement is necessary. Indeed, 328 years prior to Allen's statement, the Massachusetts Law of 1642 was an educational milestone in that for the first time in the English-speaking world, a state legislative body ruled that every child should be taught to read. As indicated by Cubberley, the Law

> '. . . directed the officials of each town [in Massachusetts] to ascertain from time to time if parents and masters were attending to their educational duties; if all children were being trained in learning and labor and other employments profitable to the Commonwealth;' and if the children were being taught 'to read and understand the principles of religion and the capital laws of the country.' (1934, p. 17)

During the more than three centuries between the Law and former Commissioner Allen, the problems of reading have been attacked with varying degrees of vigor in many different ways. The efforts have run the gamut from the stolid approaches of McGuffey; the learning-based studies of Gray, Gates, and their colleagues; to the "Madison Avenue" approach of Evelyn Wood. An examination of bibliographies of educational research reveals that more studies have been concerned with the investigation of reading than with any other single problem in education. However, one can only conclude that these scholarly attempts have been less than effective. Witness the fact that the lay population is regularly assailed by advertisements in supplements of Sunday newspapers, in pulp magazines, and even in some prestigious news magazines relating the fantastic achievements of commercial reading institutes in alleviating reading difficulties. Yet, despite the multimodal attacks, the problem remains.

The concern with improving general reading ability has radiated to concern with the ability to read materials in the different subject fields, as evidenced by the more specialized reading studies. Yet, this concern has not been the same for all the subject fields. Over the past five decades, more research investigations have been devoted to the problem of reading science materials than to any of the other fields. The reasons for the greater preoccupation with problems in reading science materials have not, to the writer's knowledge, been studied. But, there is good reason to assume that the technical vocabulary encountered in science, from the elementary- through the college-levels, is much greater and changes more frequently than that of any other field. The computer-induced knowledge explosion, which is largely in the sciences and allied fields such as engineering, may be the reason.

One may note that interest in research on reading in science has evolved through a number of periods, each with a somewhat different emphasis. The earliest reports, which appeared at the turn of the Century, dealt with the importance of meaning vocabulary. Among the more significant reports and commentaries were those of Babbitt (1907), Kirkpatrick (1907), and Doran (1907). Although these studies did refer to the sciences, they also dealt with other fields of interest and activity, including political science and the fine arts. They indicated that the breadth and impact of a student's experiences may, in a sense, be judged by the numbers and types of words to which the student attaches meaning. None of these early reports, however, took cognizance of the numbers of words that should be part of a student's meaning vocabulary. This factor was the focus of the studies carried out in the "vocabulary load" period that followed.

The "vocabulary load" period

In the two decades after the Babbitt, Kirkpatrick, and Doran studies mentioned above, very little research dealing directly with problems of reading materials in the sciences appeared. However, from about 1907-1938 a number of major vocabulary studies were undertaken and published. Among them were *qualitative* studies which sought to identify the words in, or the words which might be expected to be in, the meaning vocabularies of children and adults at various levels of maturity and *quantitative* studies which aimed at determining the *numbers* of words in these meaning vocabularies. The data for these studies were obtained from three sources: 1] analyses of children's usage of vocabulary, as reflected mainly by their written themes and by their speech; 2] adult usage of vocabulary; and 3] the vocabulary found in reading matter.

Eleven of these major studies[1] which are wholly or partly qualitative in nature served as the basis of the publication by Buckingham and Dolch, entitled *A Combined Word List* (1936). It would serve no purpose here to analyze these eleven studies individually or to present an extensive summary of their results, since these facets may readily be understood by reading *A Combined Word List* or the studies themselves. However, there are certain observations that may be made about the individual studies and the major summary of them presented by Buckingham and Dolch (1936):

1] About 19,000 words appeared in *A Combined Word List* and, on the basis of one or more of the contributing studies, 10,000 of these words were assigned grade levels of difficulty according to their usage. The problems in assigning difficulty levels according to these studies are obvious: in some studies, the dif-

---

[1]The eleven studies were carried out by Bauer (1916), the Child Study Committee of the International Kindergarten Union (1928), Gates (1926), Horn (1925), Horn (1926), Jones (1915), Payne and Garrison (1931), Studley and Ware (1914), Thorndike (1931a), Tidyman (1921), and Buckingham and Dolch's *Free Association of Children's Vocabulary* published in Buckingham and Dolch's *A Combined Word List* (1936) for the first time.

ficulty of the words was indicated only in terms of frequency of use. In addition, the words in the list fell
in two different categories, those in the "producer vocabulary" and those in the "consumer vocabulary."
The "producer vocabulary" that one uses in writing
or speaking is based mainly on recall and probably, if
used correctly, is fairly well understood. However,
the "consumer vocabulary," with which one has contact while reading materials written by others, may be
recognized, but not necessarily understood. It is obvious, therefore, that the word input for *A Combined
Word List* came from non-parallel sources.

2] The words included in "The Word List" at the end of
A Combined Word List are followed by symbols indicating their sources as well as by figures indicating the
grade-level of difficulty of the word or its frequency
of use. However, the figures assigned to the words
are not necessarily in agreement. Some words had
been assigned grade-levels of difficulty from kindergarten through the ninth grade in the different sources.
Thorndike's (1931a) study and Horn's (1926) study
listed words according to their frequency of use
namely the "thousand level" in which they were
found. Thus, it is difficult to compare this criterion
of difficulty with the criterion implied by grade-level
assignment.

3] The words in "The Word List" included the vocabulary from all fields. Some of the words could be considered part of the technical vocabulary of science,
but many could not.

Despite the weaknesses indicated above, one cannot under-
estimate the importance of the separate studies or the summary
prepared by Buckingham and Dolch (1936). For the first
time, the factor of "vocabulary load" received extensive study,
and the results of the investigations, however crude, did provide
a base for the many studies that were concurrent and the many
that followed.

Beginning in 1921, a number of concurrent studies were published in which the *quantitative* facet of vocabulary load was considered. The pioneer studies were undertaken by Thorndike and his colleagues (1921, 1924, 1931b, 1934, 1936-37), in which words were categorized according to their frequency of usage. The first Thorndike list (1921) contained the 10,000 most frequently used words in English and American literature and was synthesized from the vocabularies found in 41 different sources. The sources included children's literature; the Bible and English classics; textbooks; books about cooking, sewing, farming, and trades; newspapers; and correspondence. In this list, the words were arranged alphabetically and each was given a number indicating its frequency of appearance. Thorndike later published a second list (1931a) of about 20,000 words that was a revision and extension of the earlier one. More detailed information about these lists may be found in a major publication by Curtis (1938).

Other studies, such as those of Horn (1926) and of Ayres (1915) and Pressey (1924), were also quantitative in nature. However, the significant step was made by Thorndike and, hence, his works are emphasized here. In addition to providing information about the frequency of usage of words, Thorndike's (1921, 1924, 1931b, 1934, and 1936-37) studies were used as a basis for estimating the growth of meaning vocabulary of students at various grade levels. Table 1, based on data supplied by Thorndike (1924), indicates what this growth might be expected to be.

Table 1: Annual increases in pupils' vocabularies[a]

Grade level	Number of words
1	
2	800
3	800
4	900
5	900
6	1000
7	1100
8	1200
	1300

[a]Based on figures given by Thorndike (1924).

The studies described above and the estimates of annual growth of children's vocabulary, although intrinsically significant, had many extrinsic values. It is true that the studies dealt with general vocabulary and that their findings were not always consistent. However, they served as the basis for numerous other studies that followed whose techniques might be considered more defensible. It was from these lists that specialized word lists, such as those in the sciences, were developed. It was from the estimates of expected annual growth of vocabulary that other estimates were made for the expected growth of specialized vocabulary in the subject fields. The lists were used widely by authors to determine the words that might reasonably be used in writing textbooks and by teachers to measure the level of reading difficulty of written material. The implications of these studies for further research in the development of science vocabulary is discussed later in this paper.

Vocabulary load and the teaching of science

The role of Teachers College, Columbia University, and of Thorndike's studies in the investigation of problems of reading science materials is evident when one analyzes the early research studies. Lively and Pressey (1923) studied the vocabulary of 18 science texts including two texts from general science and one each from biology, chemistry, college physics, and physiology. They derived a vocabulary list by taking one line per page from enough pages throughout each text to make up a 1,000 word list. They then determined the numbers of different words in the 1,000 word samples, referring to these numbers as the "vocabulary ranges" of the textbooks. The words were compared with the rankings of the words in Thorndike's 10,000 word list and values for the vocabulary burdens were obtained. Lively and Pressey's research was the first designed specifically to measure "vocabulary load" in textbooks in science.

A number of investigators, (e.g., Curtis, 1924, 1926; Powers, 1925) questioned the use of the words contained in the

Thorndike lists for evaluating the difficulty of specialized reading material. They challenged two of the basic premises underlying Thorndike's efforts: 1] that there is a high negative relationship between the difficulty of the word and the frequency of its use and 2] that the sources from which Thorndike compiled his list were representative of written materials that people ordinarily read. These premises were questioned particularly by researchers in the sciences because Thorndike compiled his list were representative of written vocabulary rather than vocabulary of specialized fields.

This latter challenge was probably the motivation for a study at Teachers College, Columbia University, undertaken by Curtis (1924). In his study, Curtis investigated the scientific terms found among more than one-quarter million words in 630 articles that appeared in two weeks' issues of six representative daily newspapers. He used the Thorndike list as a criterion for judging the importance and difficulty of the scientific terms he had isolated. He found that nearly one-third of the scientific terms appearing in the articles were not included in the Thorndike list (Curtis, 1924; 1926). Curtis concluded:

> It would seem . . . that the addition to the child's vocabulary of each thousand of the most frequently occurring words does not add greatly to his equipment for an intelligent reading in the public press, and that . . . vocabulary building based upon *The Teacher's Word Book* does not in itself promise to provide adequately for the needs of pupils in science. . . . (1924, p. 12)

The inadequacies of the Thorndike list discovered by Curtis stimulated extensive research activity. It is interesting to note that the need for developing appropriate specialized vocabularies led to the use of "term," such as "scientific term," for words in the specialized vocabularies ("word" was used to designate words found in the general vocabulary).

Powers (1925), a colleague of Curtis' at Teachers College, Columbia University, undertook extensive investigations to identify scientific terms to supplement the 10,000 words in the earlier Thorndike list. With his assistants, Powers analyzed two textbooks in general science, two in chemistry, and five in biology and listed all the words appearing in them. More than a total of a million words were listed (obviously, with many repetitions). The individual words were matched against those appearing in Thorndike's list. Powers' list was later supplemented by adding words found in one additional textbook for biology, two textbooks for physics, three science tradebooks, and a number of miscellaneous materials, including over fifty articles on science from magazines. Powers found that nearly 14,000 words contained in his list were not included in the Thorndike list. Powers' list was then reduced by eliminating compound words and hyphenated words, finally producing a list of 1,828 scientific terms that appeared in fewer than ten of the sources. The final list of terms was assumed to contain those which might reasonably be considered to be part of the common technical vocabulary of science.

The major studies that followed, however, were undertaken by Curtis in the fields of general science, biology, and chemistry. These studies were the basis for Curtis' (1938) major publication entitled *Investigations of Vocabulary in Textbooks of Science for Secondary Schools*. In this, Curtis analyzed the findings of 46 published studies involving reading and 67 unpublished studies, mainly master's theses some of which he directed at the University of Michigan. On the basis of these studies, Curtis came to the following conclusions:

1] The textbooks for junior high and senior high school science contained many technical terms and non-technical words that were beyond the common vocabularies of the students.

2] In general, in junior high and senior high school science textbooks, more words found at the 7,000-word level of Thorndike's list were not understood than words at any preceding level. Thus, Curtis assumed that this was the criterion level at which authors should begin to simplify the vocabulary they used in writing their textbooks.

3] The numbers of technical terms and nontechnical words found in science textbooks and which students do not comprehend, increased rapidly beyond the 7,000-word level in Thorndike's list. This finding suggests that authors tended to overestimate the level of vocabulary comprehension of students for whom the books were designed.

4] The difficulties students had with word comprehension were found more frequently with words within the word list prepared by Thorndike than with words not included within the word list. Thus, authors tended to use words that had a relatively high frequency of usage rather than esoteric terms.

5] At both the junior high and senior high school levels the difficulties students had with reading science materials were caused by nontechnical words rather than by scientific terms. Thus, it would seem reasonable that greater emphasis should have been placed on using a simpler nontechnical vocabulary.

These conclusions served as a basis for further analyses in master's theses dealing with science vocabulary and for the direct efforts of Curtis' graduate students at the University of Michigan in developing lists of terms appropriate for the teaching of different science courses. Some of the studies Curtis directed were conducted by Adams (1935), Anderson (1936), Eaton (1938), Fisher (1938), and Hart (1936). These, plus several others described in Curtis' (1938) major publication, dealt with glossary terms for courses in general science, biology, and chemistry. Surprisingly, there was little evidence of interest on the part of his graduate students or other researchers in developing similar glossary lists for physics.

In essence, the studies cited above which Curtis directed involved the tabulations of the glossaries in textbooks that were then current in the three fields mentioned. The terms from the glossaries were tabulated and submitted to judges for their evaluation. They were instructed to evaluate the terms obtained from the glossaries on the basis of their being "essential," "desirable," or "neither essential nor desirable," in the respective courses.

Although the detailed findings of the investigations by Curtis' graduate students are far too voluminous to describe here, it was found that the agreement among the judges concerning "essential" terms was not great. In order to validate the findings further, the lists were then sent to a number of teachers of science for additional evaluation. The glossaries of terms that emerged from the evaluations appear in Curtis' (1938) work.

Obviously, some of the terms that appeared in these early lists are still valid, although the knowledge explosion has rendered many of them less relevant. In addition, the vast number of new scientific terms that have been generated since the earlier studies are not included. Thus, these lists are currently only of historical use. Unfortunately, the extensive research that culminated in Curtis' (1938) work was curtailed severely during World War II. After World War II, investigations in this area were resumed and a number of major concerns were raised about the earlier studies. Some of these concerns were:

1] A search of the literature failed to reveal any studies that indicated the number of new scientific terms for which a student should acquire meanings at the different grade levels. Any suggestions of numbers in the literature are purely conjecture.

2] The meaning of "comprehension" of a scientific term had not been clearly defined. Some writers apparently equated a satisfactory definition of a term with comprehension. Others disagreed, indicating that an understanding of the *concept* related to the term was indicative of comprehension.

3] It was generally agreed that an author could use many appropriate nontechnical words and scientific terms in his books and yet the materials might be written poorly and so be complicated and difficult to comprehend.

For about five years after World War II, textbook publishers still depended on the different word lists and lists of glossary terms for evaluating reading difficulty of the materials they published. However, by 1950, it was generally recognized that the pattern of writing, as well as the terms used, was a criterion of reading difficulty. Thus, the period of the "reading formulae" came into being.

The "reading formulae" period

After World War II, with few exceptions, most reading research with science materials involved measurements of reading difficulty and most of these measurements employed reading formulae. Measuring reading difficulty by comparing the vocabulary of science materials with word lists for all practical purposes disappeared. Generally, the various formulae developed took cognizance in different ways of three major factors: 1] the number of words in the sentences of the samples analyzed; 2] the difficulty of the words as measured by the number of syllables they contained; and 3] the number of personal references such as "I," "you" and "they" in the sentences. It was assumed that the first two factors increased reading difficulty, whereas the latter factor reduced it.

Many different reading formulae were developed, although the five used most frequently in published studies were those developed by Flesch (1946), Yoakam (1945), Lorge (1944), Dale and Chall (1948), and Spache (1953). The Spache formula was designed mainly for use with materials for grades one through three while the Yoakam formula and the Lorge formula were designed for the upper-elementary grades (although the Lorge formula was also found to be useful for materials designed for the junior and senior high school). Both the Flesch and Dale-Chall formulae were designed for analyzing the difficulty of reading materials ranging from the fourth grade through the college level.

The earliest and most extensive group of studies using reading formulae designed to measure the reading difficulty of science materials were undertaken by Mallinson and his colleagues

(Mallinson, Sturm, and Patton, 1950; Mallinson, Sturm, and Mallinson, 1950a, 1950b, 1952a, 1952b, 1952c, 1954, 1957). They were concerned with textbooks designed for science courses from the elementary through the high school levels. The same techniques were followed in all studies in the series. First, all the publishers of science textbooks for the respective levels and courses were contacted to obtain copies of the most recent editions. The experience of the investigators indicated that all the textbooks that were then available were obtained. Since an analysis of all the textual material in all the textbooks was impractical, it was decided to use a modification of the sampling technique suggested by Flesch for use with his formula. Hence, it was decided to select from each textbook for the purposes of analyses one sample passage for each 100 pages or fraction thereof, but not less than five passages from any one textbook. The number of pages in each text was computed by counting from the first page designated by an Arabic numeral to the last page of the last chapter. Pages upon which appeared chapter endings, supplementary activities, and questions were included in the count. The pages containing the indices, glossaries, and tables of contents were excluded. The number of pages thus computed in each textbook was then divided by the number of samples to be taken from the respective textbook. In this way, each textbook was divided into sections of an equal number of pages. A page was then selected from each of the sections by using a table of random numbers.

A 100-word sample was taken from each page thus selected by counting from the first word of the first new paragraph on that page. If the page contained no reading material, the sample was selected from the next page that did. The legends under the illustrations on the pages selected were disregarded. These samples were then analyzed using the Flesch (1946) formula.

The reading difficulty scores obtained by using the Flesch formula were converted into a grade-level value of reading difficulty by means of what Belden and Lee (1962) referred to as the "Mallinson criterion."[2] The findings of these studies by Mallinson and his coworkers were essentially the same, except for the textbooks in the fields of physics and chemistry, for which the first conclusion did not apply:

1] The levels of reading difficulty of many textbooks in science were found to be too high for the students for whom the textbooks were designed.

2] The differences between the levels of reading difficulty of the easiest and the most difficult textbooks analyzed in all the studies were both statistically significant and consequential.

3] In some science textbooks, whose average level of reading difficulty seemed satisfactory, there were passages that would have been difficult even for some college students.

4] Many science textbooks contained nontechnical words that could have been replaced by easier synonyms.

5] Little cognizance seemed to have been taken of growth in reading ability during the school year, since the earlier portions of some of the textbooks were difficult, whereas the latter portions were easier.

In general, textbooks for chemistry and physics were not likely to be as difficult to read for the students for whom they were designed as the science textbooks at the earlier levels. Also, the most popular textbooks (popular in the sense of being used frequently in the school systems) were found in the easiest and middle groups with respect to level of reading difficulty. There were, however, two textbooks for high school physics and one textbook in high school chemistry that might have been difficult for college students.

Studies dealing mainly with the level of reading difficulty of science textbooks, other than those just mentioned, did not

---

[2] The "Mallinson criterion" is basically a modification of Flesch's conversion table (Mallinson, Sturm, and Patton, 1950).

begin to appear until after 1960. Belden and Lee (1961) undertook a study, one facet of which was to determine the level of reading difficulty of five textbooks for general biology that were adopted for use in the Oklahoma high schools, using the Dale-Chall formula. Their findings indicated that only one of the five textbooks had a readability level suitable for at least fifty per cent of the students for whom they were designed.

Belden and Lee (1962) undertook a similar study for five textbooks for high school chemistry and five textbooks for high school physics. They claimed that their findings for the chemistry textbooks were different from those of Mallinson, Sturm, and Mallinson (1952b), indicating that only half the textbooks, at best, were suitable with respect to reading difficulty for the students for whom they were designed. Their findings for textbooks of physics, however, supported those of Mallinson, Sturm, and Mallinson (1952c), namely that four of the textbooks of physics had readability scores below the usual twelfth-grade placement of physics courses.

Denslow (1961), Newport (1965), and Ottley (1965) were concerned with the evaluation of the level of reading difficulty of textbooks for elementary science. Denslow, using the Spache (1953) formula, evaluated eight science textbooks for use in the first grade published from 1957-1961. He also made word counts of the vocabulary in these texts. The investigator found 61 words, which were termed "basic," that were common to all eight textbooks studied and, like Mallinson, Sturm, and Patton (1950), found a wide range in level of reading difficulty. One may question this study, however, in that first graders are not generally expected to read science textbooks independently. Ordinarily the materials are read in small group sessions or in a general class session with help from the teacher.

Newport's (1965) study dealt with the level of reading difficulty of nine series of textbooks for elementary science for grades one through six. The Spache (1953) formula was used for the textbooks for grades one through three and the Yoakam (1945) formula was used for textbooks from grades four through six. Newport concluded that the readability levels of the textbooks for the primary grades were suitable for most of the students for whom they were designed. Those designed for the intermediate grades varied greatly in reading difficulty, although, in general, the levels of reading difficulty were higher than might be desired. The textbooks for the upper grades were not found to be so difficult.

Ottley (1965) used the Lorge (1944) formula to determine the readability of science textbooks for grades four, five, and six published between 1959 and 1962. His findings were similar to those of Newport (1965), namely that the levels of reading difficulty of the fourth-grade science textbooks were too high; those designed for fifth grade were less difficult; whereas those designed for sixth-grade level seemed to be most suitable.

One study undertaken by Major and Collette (1961) used the Flesch (1946) formula to evaluate the readability level of college textbooks for general biology. They concluded that the most widely used college textbooks for general biology were written beyond the level of comprehension of college students, mainly because of the polysyllabic nature of the words used in the texts.

The last study that seems to be of sufficient significance to report here was conducted by Jacobson (1965) who investigated the reading difficulty of textbooks of chemistry and physics used in Minnesota. The materials for analysis were selected from 16 textbooks for high school chemistry and physics including three textbooks from college chemistry courses, three from college physics courses, and one from high school physical science courses. Ten 200-word samples were selected from each textbook and the word difficulty was defined as number of words indicated by students in chemistry and physics as being difficult. An extensive statistical analysis was undertaken with the data thus obtained. It was concluded that the levels of reading difficulty of the textbooks varied widely; many of them were too difficult for the students for whom they were designed.

The "reading formulae" phase of research, however, seems

now to have disappeared as has the "vocabulary load" phase. The reasons are manifold, but among the most important are these:

1] In the early 1950's Flesch (1951) recognized that his first formula failed to consider what might be called "interesting writing style." Obviously, materials having the same measured reading difficulty might vary greatly with respect to their being "interesting" or "dull." Thus, Flesch attempted to develop a measure for the level of interest of written material as well as for the traditional facets of reading difficulty. Efforts with his formula have been disappointing and little use of it has been made by investigators. Only one study of significance, that of Crooks and Smith (1957), evaluated science textbooks using the "Flesch Human Interest Scale." The investigators selected twenty widely used textbooks—17 in various areas of college biology and 3 in the physical sciences —and analyzed them both with respect to reading difficulty and "interest." They found that two of the textbooks were "fairly difficult" while the rest were "difficult." However, all twenty science textbooks were judged to be "dull" which somehow causes one to question the "Scale."

2] In the later 1950's, great emphasis began to be placed on the "Inquiry Approach" to teaching science, for which the materials did not have a narrative format like that of the more traditional textbooks. More "lab texts" were, and are, being published. Thus, the appropriateness of reading formulae for assessing the reading difficulty of these materials has been questioned.

3] The advent of television had an impact on the development of vocabulary of students which, to this day, has not been fully studied.

Research in reading in science since the late 1950's has

failed to evidence any clearcut pattern or direction. Some of the studies discussed in the next section of this paper are indicative of the "search" for a new direction in this area of reading research.

Seeking directions for research in science

As early as 1954, the validity of using reading formulae for measuring reading difficulty was challenged. On February 15, 1954, at the Convention of the American Educational Research Association, in the Hotel Traymore in Atlantic City, Dr. Emmett A. Betts, then at Temple University, challenged the need for laborious investigations with reading formulae. He stated that "any elementary teacher can estimate the reading difficulty of a passage from a textbook." There was, of course, no evidence to support or negate such an assumption. Hence, Mallinson and Holmes (1958) sought to obtain evidence using the passages that had been selected for analysis in the earlier studies of elementary and junior high school textbooks by Mallinson and his colleagues (Mallinson, Sturm, and Patton, 1950; Mallinson, Sturm, and Mallinson, 1950b; 1952a).

The Flesch (1946), Lorge (1944), and Dale-Chall (1948) were used to assess the reading difficulty of 199 sample reading passages from textbooks of science for grades four through eight. The samples to be measured were assembled into packets of twenty by means of a random selection of samples from the 199 passages. Packets were then sent to 36 teachers classified as "reading experts" or "specialists in reading" in certain larger midwestern cities. These persons were requested to estimate the level of reading difficulty of each of the reading passages by visual inspection and to indicate their estimates by checking the appropriate blanks on a form supplied. The procedure was repeated, except that two elementary teachers in each of the school systems, not classified as "reading experts" or "specialists in reading," were asked to undertake the task. A comparison between the consistency of measurements between the three formulae and the estimates of the "reading experts" and classroom teachers was then made. The median difference for measurements in reading difficulty with the formulae was found to be 1.0 years; for reading expert, 3.0 years; and for elementary classroom teachers, 4.0 years. This study indicated conclusively that reading formulae could be used with validity to measure reading difficulty insofar as the concept of reading difficulty as exemplified by these formulae is defensible. It also indicated that the estimates of reading experts and teachers differ far more than measurements made with formulae. However, this study did not provide any evidence about factors related to reading difficulty other than those included in the formulae such as the interest level of the material.

It was during the later portion of the "reading formulae" period that the factor of reading interest began to draw attention. Barnes, Beck, Reiner, and Washton (1958) developed a list of criteria for selecting supplementary science books for gifted high school students. The list was developed from responses to a questionnaire submitted to 150 members of the National Association for Research in Science Teaching. The six most important criteria with respect to "effect on the reader" thus identified were these: "It provokes thinking and discussion;" "It develops interest in matters of science;" "It stimulates further reading;" "It helps to articulate and elucidate scientific concepts and principles;" "It suggests further problems;" and "It gives insights into social implications and contributions of science." The six most important criteria with respect to "qualities of the book" were: "It is accurate and authoritative;" "It is fair and sincere in its presentation of controversial subject matter;" "Its enrichment material goes beyond that of secondary textbooks;" "It has good literary standards;" "Its general theme and tone are wholesome;" and "It is a book of lasting value—worth owning." However, the study indicated also that the criteria for selection applied about as well for all students in secondary schools as they did to the intellectually gifted.

Despite the efforts involved in completing the Barnes, Beck,

Reiner, and Washton study and despite the fact that it received financial support from the Library of Science of New York City, there is little evidence that its findings have been put to great use. One may suggest that the ongoing program of the American Association for the Advancement of Science, in reviewing tradebooks for various scientific fields and publishing the reviews in the publication, *Science Books—A Quarterly Review,* has supplanted this as well as similar efforts.

There have been a few research studies concerned with the general area of "scientific literacy" (the ability of an intelligent layman to read scientific literature and understand its implications for the culture), although together it is difficult to ascertain that these studies point to a new direction in research in reading in science. Four were undertaken by Shores and his colleagues (Shores and Saupe, 1953; Shores, 1960a; 1960b; 1961). In the earliest study, Shores and Saupe (1953) attempted to determine the relationship between the Test of Reading for Problem-solving in Science and other measures such as mental age, reading age, arithmetic age, and socioeconomic status. The study revealed little that had not been known earlier, namely that ability to read in science was related to general reading ability and to mental ability.

Two of the studies (Shores, 1960a; 1960b) dealt with the perceptions of sixth graders when their purposes for reading science materials were directed in certain ways. It was discovered that adults were far more able than sixth graders to adjust their reading habits when specific purposes were indicated and that sixth graders were generally unclear as to how to read for different purposes. Shores also found that the purposes for reading influenced the reading rate of sixth graders and that the scores obtained on reading tests are not necessarily good predictors of the ideas that sixth graders obtained from their reading.

In his final study, Shores (1961) compared the relationship between reading rate and comprehension of 46 sixth-grade pupils and 51 able adult readers. In general, he found that more rapid readers are likely to score higher on standardized tests of reading than are slower readers, but that there is little relationship between reading rate and comprehension of more difficult scientific material.

In another study Marshall (1962) sought to determine how well the Flesch formula would predict comprehension of a passage on electricity in a high school textbook. Two hundred physics students were separated into four groups on the basis of scores obtained on tests of reading and physics. Half the students then read an original textbook passage and the other half read a rewritten passage, covering the same material but having a high level of reading difficulty. No significant relationship was indicated between the level of readability and the comprehension of the material by the students. It was concluded, therefore, that the use of the Flesch formula for measuring the level of difficulty of textbooks in high school physics was irrelevant.

As indicated earlier, the two significant periods in research in reading in science are the "vocabulary load" period and the "reading formulae" period. The published material of the last decade consists mainly of a few studies using reading formulae and a few other unrelated studies apparently groping with reading comprehension in the sciences and what is frequently termed "scientific literacy." Unfortunately, the latter term is as yet ill-defined.

Needs and future directions for reading research in science

In attempting to look to the future, draw certain conclusions, and make recommendations for further studies, several points seem worthy of mention:

1] A search of the literature and a perusal of the titles of papers presented at professional meetings indicate a great decline in the past decade in the numbers of research investigations dealing with problems of reading in science. The writer has noted this personally as

Editor of *School Science and Mathematics* and as a member of, and attendee at, the Conventions of the National Council on Measurements in Education, the American Educational Research Association, the American Association for the Advancement of Science, and the National Association for Research in Science Teaching.

2] From the few studies undertaken in recent years, it is difficult to ascertain any direction. Few research investigations appear to be replications, extensions, or corollaries of other studies of the period. In short, they appear to be flying off in all directions.

In searching for reasons for the two situations mentioned above, two points discussed earlier in this paper may serve to suggest partial answers for the phenomenon as well as to point out future directions for research. They are:

1] The impact of commercial television on the scientific awareness and sophistication of students.

2] The newer "inquiry oriented" programs of science instruction and the reduction of "read about" approaches to science teaching at all levels.

In the future, it seems reasonable that research related to reading in science may well focus on questions and problems such as:

1] How has the growth in students' "consumer vocabulary" resulting from commercial television viewing and other modern communication systems affected their ability to read science materials? In other words, what effect, if any, does viewing a live telecast from the moon have on a student's ability to read and understand an astronomy book written at his level?

2] Have the newer curriculum materials that attempt to make students "inquirers" in science, rather than "readers about" science taken cognizance of problems of reading? In other words, unless students can read the "foci" for inquiry and understand the task, can they really develop skills of inquiry? Further, do they possess the "producer vocabulary" to express their answers or partial answers discovered through the inquiry process?

In summary, then, although several factors have apparently resulted in a temporary dearth of research studies related to problems of reading in science, they may well have opened many new avenues in the future for productive and meaningful studies.

References

Adams, L. P. An analysis of twelve general science and biology glossaries to determine the words essential for understanding, or desirable for enriching, these courses. Unpublished master's thesis, University of Michigan, 1935.

Anderson, W. H. An investigation of Adams's list of general science words and an investigation of the scientific words appearing in newspapers. Unpublished master's thesis, University of Michigan, 1936.

Ayres, L. P. *A measuring scale for ability in spelling.* New York: Russell Sage Foundation Division of Education, 1915.

Babbitt, E. H. A vocabulary test. *Popular Science Monthly*, 1907, *70*, 378.

Barnes, C. W., Beck, A. D., Reiner, W. B., and Washton, N. S. Criteria for selecting supplementary reading science books for intellectually gifted high school students. *Science Education*, 1958, *42*, 215-18.

Bauer, N. *The New Orleans public school spelling list.* New Orleans: F. F. Hansel and Brothers, 1916.

Belden, B. R., and Lee, W. D. Readability of biology textbooks and the reading ability of biology students. *School Science and Mathematics*, 1961, *61*, 689-93.

Belden, B. R., and Lee, W. D. Textbook readability and reading ability of science students. *Science Teacher*, 1962, *29*, 20-21.

Buckingham, B. R., and Dolch, E. W. *A combined word list.* Boston: Ginn, 1936.

Child Study Committee of the International Kindergarten Union. *A study of the vocabulary of children before entering the first grade.* Washington, D. C.: The International Kindergarten Union, 1928.

Crooks, K. B. M., and Smith, C. H. The reading problem in college science instruction. *Science Education*, 1957, *41*, 54-57.

Cubberley, E. P. *Public education in the United States: a study and interpretation of American educational history.* Boston: Houghton, Mifflin, 1934.

Curtis, F. D. Some values derived from extensive reading of general science. *Teachers College Contributions to Education*, 1924, No. 163.

Curtis, F. D. A study of the vocabulary of scientific articles appearing in daily newspapers. *School and Society*, 1926, *23*, 821-24.

Curtis, F. D. *Investigation of vocabulary in textbooks of science for secondary schools.* Boston: Ginn, 1938.

Dale, E., and Chall, Jeanne S. A formula for predicting readability: instructions. *Educational Research Bulletin*, 1948, *27*, 37-54.

Denslow, O. D. Vocabulary and sentence study of eight first grade science books. *Elementary English,* 1961, *38,* 487-90.

Doran, E. W. A study of vocabularies. *Pedagogical Seminary,* 1907, *14,* 401-38.

Eaton, H. S. An investigation of the vocabulary difficulty encountered by pupils in reading a textbook of high-school chemistry, and an investigation of the scientific terms acceptable for inclusion in a textbook of general science or biology. Unpublished master's thesis, University of Michigan, 1938.

Fisher, J. An investigation of the terms to be included in the glossary of a textbook of chemistry for high-school use. Unpublished master's thesis, University of Michigan, 1938.

Flesch, R. *The art of plain talk.* New York: Harper and Brothers, 1946.

Flesch, R. *How to test readability.* New York: Harper and Brothers, 1951.

Gates, A. I. *A reading vocabulary for the primary grades.* New York: Teachers College, Columbia University, 1926.

Hart, W. G. An investigation of scientific terms taken from newspapers, and an investigation of the scientific terms desirable for inclusion in a textbook of biology. Unpublished master's thesis, University of Michigan, 1936.

Horn, E. The commonest words in the spoken vocabulary of children up to and including six years of age. *Yearbook of the National Society for the Study of Education,* 1925, *24* (1), Chapter VII.

Horn, E. A basic writing vocabulary. *University of Iowa Monographs in Education, First Series,* 1926, No. 4.

Jacobson, M. D. Reading difficulty of physics and chemistry textbooks. *Educational and Psychological Measurement,* 1965, *25,* 449-57.

Jones, W. F. A concrete investigation of the material of English spelling. *Unpublished manuscript,* University of South Dakota, Vermillion, South Dakota, 1915.

Kirkpatrick, E. A. A vocabulary test. *Popular Science Monthly,* 1907, *70,* 157-64.

Lively, Bertha A., and Pressey, S. L. A method for measuring the 'vocabulary burden' of textbooks. *Educational Administration and Supervision,* 1923, *9,* 389-98.

Lorge, I. Predicting readability. *Teachers College Record,* 1944, *45,* 404-19.

Major, A. G., and Collette, A. T. The readability of college general biology textbooks. *Science Education,* 1961, *45,* 216-24.

Mallinson, G. G., and Holmes, Roma Herrington. A study of the ability of teachers to estimate the reading difficulty of materials for elementary science. *Fifteenth Yearbook of the National Council on Measurements Used in Education,* 1958, *15,* 105-08.

Mallinson, G. G., Sturm, H. E., and Mallinson, Lois M. The reading difficulty of textbooks for high-school biology. *American Biology Teacher,* 1950, *12,* 151-56. (a)

Mallinson, G. G., Sturm, H. E., and Mallinson, Lois M. The reading difficulty of textbooks in junior-high-school science. *School Review,* 1950, *58,* 536-40. (b)

Mallinson, G. G., Sturm, H. E., and Mallinson, Lois M. The reading difficulty of textbooks for general science. *School Review,* 1952, *60,* 94-98. (a)

Mallinson, G. G., Sturm, H. E., and Mallinson, Lois M. The reading difficulty of textbooks for high-school chemistry. *Journal of Chemical Education,* 1952, *29,* 629-31. (b)

Mallinson, G. G., Sturm, H. E., and Mallinson, Lois M. The reading difficulty of textbooks for high-school physics. *Science Education,* 1952, *36,* 19-23. (c)

Mallinson, G. G., Sturm, H. E., and Mallinson, Lois M. The reading difficulty of textbooks for general physical science and earth science. *School Science and Mathematics,* 1954, *54,* 612-16.

Mallinson, G. G., Sturm, H. E., and Mallinson, Lois M. The reading difficulty of some recent textbooks for science. *School Science and Mathematics,* 1957, *57,* 364-66.

Mallinson, G. G., Sturm, H. E., and Patton, R. E. The reading difficulty of textbooks in elementary science. *Elementary School Journal,* 1950, *50,* 460-63.

Marshall, J. S. Comprehension and alleged readability of high school physics textbooks. *Science Education,* 1962, *46,* 335-46.

Newport, J. F. The readability of science textbooks for elementary schools. *Elementary School Journal,* 1965, *66,* 40-43.

Ottley, L. Readability of science textbooks for grades four, five, and six. *School Science and Mathematics,* 1965, *65,* 363-66.

Payne, B. R., and Garrison, S. C. *Payne-Garrison speller.* Chicago: Rand McNally, 1931.

Powers, S. R. A vocabulary of high school science textbooks. *Teachers College Record,* 1925, *26,* 368-92.

Pressey, Luella C. The determination of the technical vocabularies of the school subjects. *School and Society,* 1924, *20,* 91-96.

Shores, J. H. Reading of science for two separate purposes as perceived by sixth grade students and able adult readers. *Elementary English,* 1960, *37,* 461-68. (a)

Shores, J. H. Reading science materials for two distinct purposes. *Elementary English,* 1960, *37,* 546-53. (b)

Shores, J. H. Are fast readers the best readers?—a second report. *Elementary English,* 1961, *38,* 236-45.

Shores, J. H., and Saupe, J. L. Reading for problem-solving in science. *Journal of Educational Psychology,* 1953, *44,* 149-58.

Spache, G. D. A new readability formula for primary grade reading materials. *Elementary School Journal,* 1953, *53,* 410-13.

Studley, C. K., and Ware, A. Common essentials in spelling. Chico, California: State Normal School, *Bulletin No. 7,* 1914.

Thorndike, E. L. *The teacher's word book.* New York: Bureau of Publications, Teachers College, Columbia University, 1921.

Thorndike, E. L. The vocabularies of school pupils. *Contributions to Education,* Vol. I. Yonkers-on-Hudson, New York: World Book, 1924.

Thorndike, E. L. *A teacher's word book of 20,000 words.* New York: Teachers College, Columbia University, 1931. (a)

Thorndike, E. L. *A teacher's word book of the 20,000 words found most frequently and widely in general reading for children and young people.* New York: Bureau of Publications, Teachers College, Columbia University, 1931. (b)

Thorndike, E. L. Improving the ability to read. *Teachers College Record,* 1934, *36,* 1-19, 123-44, 229-41.

Thorndike, E. L. The vocabulary of books for children in grades three to eight. *Teachers College Record,* 1936-37, *38,* 196-205, 316-23, 416-29.

Thorndike, E. L. The vocabularies of school pupils. *Contributions to Education,* Vol. I, Yonkers-on-Hudson, New York: World Book, 1924. Cited by G. G. Mallinson. Some problems of vocabulary and reading difficulty in teaching junior high school science. *School Science and Mathematics,* 1952, *52,* 269-74.

Tidyman, W. F. *A survey of the writing vocabularies of public school children in Connecticut.* United States Bureau of Education, Teacher's Leaflet No. 15, 1921.

Yoakam, G. A. Reading difficulty of school textbooks. *Elementary English Review,* 1945, *22,* 304-09, 333-36.

Carl Bernard Smith

Reading in the sciences:
Classroom implications

The teaching of science content reading suffers similar ailments with all the content subjects. There is confusion over who is responsible for reading instruction, what meaning research has for this instruction, and how one instructs. These concerns affect both elementary and secondary science teachers, who may be doing an excellent job teaching science content but who often lack training in how to teach the reading of science content.

The purpose of this paper is to examine the research presented in the preceding paper (the Mallinson review of research related to reading science), to see what implications there are for both the scope of and the methodology of teaching science content reading, and to identify those areas where research efforts ought to be focused for more adequate treatment of the problem. The paper also suggests ways that the classroom teacher can make the teaching of science content reading more effective.

What research says
Readability

In the previous paper, the research related to the readability of science material was reviewed and there were identified two important considerations for teachers: 1] The vocabulary load, both technical and nontechnical, of science texts is quite different from the vocabulary taught in the elementary school reading program, and many words differ likewise from the 20,000 most frequently used words as displayed in the Thorndike list.   2] The readability of science texts generally measures much higher than the reading level of the students for whom the texts were designed.

One of Mallinson's reported findings concerning vocabulary load may come as a surprise to some teachers. It was noted that students at the junior and senior high school levels had greater difficulties in comprehending the nontechnical words in their science books than they had in comprehending the technical terms. Unaware of this fact, teachers who teach concepts and vocabulary as a prelude to reading and understanding the science material ordinarily concentrate on the new scientific terms to the exclusion of the other vocabulary. Supposedly, since the scientific terms are clearly relevant to the development of the theme of the text, both the student and the teacher concentrate on identifying and conceptualizing those terms. But if science writers are including large numbers of difficult nontechnical words, they are increasing the density of the concepts and also magnifying the problem of word identification and understanding. For that reason it seems that text writers should use a simpler nontechnical vocabulary and that teachers should search out words that might interfere with comprehension, no matter what their character.

Mallinson noted another finding that classroom teachers ought to keep in mind: even those texts that had an average reading difficulty score and that seemed satisfactory for the intended grade level included some sections which were quite difficult.

Word analysis

Since science content seems fraught with vocabulary problems, several investigators have explored ways of overcoming them. Severson (1963) worked with tenth-grade biology classes in an experimental word analysis and vocabulary development program. This program increased achievement 17 per cent over the control group on a biology test. Stauffer's (1966) analysis of middle-grade content texts led him to conclude that to help children through these texts, a word skill program that emphasizes both meaning and a phonetic-structural attack should be used. What Severson and Stauffer recommended is corroborated by the evidence from a study by Aldridge and Anderson (1960) who found that science reading was related most intensely to abilities in word usage; least intensely to abilities in math computation and English grammar usage. Aldridge and Anderson concluded that the students' abilities to know the meaning and to identify the form of words enable them to solve at least one of the basic problems associated with reading science and to score somewhat higher, therefore, on science tests.

But vocabulary is only one reading problem area. Several additional studies on text-related problems in the teaching of science merit consideration because of their direction for teaching. Some pertinent studies are related to author writing style, student interest in the style and content, the purpose for reading, the organizational structure of the selection, and typographical aids.

Writing style

As was indicated in the Mallinson review, readability formulas are limited in their analysis of the difficulty of a selection. For example, one factor that they do not measure, at least not overtly, is writing style. The way a writer expresses his ideas can vary infinitely. Involved are such factors as sentence length, density of concepts, and the use of imagery and connotative words.[1]

Working on the premise that style is a major factor in textbook readability, Williams (1964) rewrote passages from a

---

[1]Density of concepts refers to the compactness of ideas, the number of different concepts contained within a sentence. Imagery means picture-making devices (He ran like a hippopotamus.), and connotative words refer to those that carry personal and emotional content beyond the dictionary definition. These factors refer only to sentence construction and do not include a broader style consideration, that of how a writer organizes his information and progresses from one idea to another. Specific examples of style are presented in the following section.

sixth-grade science text and found that a simplification of the style and of the nontechnical vocabulary increased both rate and comprehension for sixth-grade learners. Hill (1967) found that in other studies with rewritten texts similar improvement was noted. Since it is not feasible that teachers rewrite their science texts, Hill recommended that schools develop a systematic program of instruction in comprehension and study skills for mastery of content subjects. Students would thus be given specific direction and practice in learning to compensate for the style and density of concepts presented in their books. They could learn aids such as using the lead sentence in each paragraph for obtaining an overview of the content and for asking specific questions; or using the SQ3R study approach: Survey the selection; establish Questions to search for; Read carefully; Recite what you have read; Review to establish the reliability of your recitation. Another way teachers can deal with material that appears quite difficult is to list the important concepts and then teach them with related readings that are simpler.

Student interest

Related to writing style, but not totally tied to it, is the matter of the reader's interest in the textual material. In a study of twenty popular college science texts, all twenty were classified as dull according to the Flesch Human Interest Scale (Crooks and Smith, 1957). This finding would presumably be true at the elementary and secondary levels also. While values and attitudes naturally affect a reader's reaction to the content he reads and, to a degree, his comprehension of that content (Groff, 1962), the reader would have to possess extremely high intrinsic motivation to read and comprehend well in material which the style makes dull. It would be folly for a writer at any level to assume that the reader's intrinsic motivation would overcome his own lack of imagination in presenting a message. Given dull writing, however, the teacher needs to take special pains to pose advance questions and problems, assign projects, and bring in related material so that the concepts do not die because the manner of presentation has no life.

This plea for an appealing writing style is not to suggest that students need a narrative or story-line approach in order to be interested in science reading. In fact, Blue (1964) reported that seventh graders actually prefer an expository style to a narrative, because the former promises them more condensed information—a value that appeals to them. But the writer of science texts and the teacher who selects those texts must remember that an appealing style can do much to win an apathetic reader.

While it is virtually impossible to specifically and accurately define and/or assess a writing style that appeals to all students, a general guideline can be offered. Lengthy, complex sentences filled with abstract terms are usually more difficult to read than shorter sentences that contain concrete pictures. Concrete writing is generally more palatable and comprehensible than the abstract kind. Consider these examples of abstract and concrete:

1] Evaporation is the process whereby the liquid state of matter is changed into gases which are dissipated into the atmosphere.

2] Water, gasoline, and other liquids sometimes seem to disappear. Actually the liquids change into gases which escape into the air. That chemical change is called evaporation.

Purpose for reading

Regardless of how readable a style may be, the competent reader is able to shift his reading rate to accommodate the purpose for which he is reading. He can whisk briskly across an introduction if his only purpose is to glean the main idea, but if he wants to study a chemical bond concept, he can proceed slowly, weighing and sorting ideas as he goes. It seems, however, that adjusting rate to purpose in science reading does not occur atuomatically. In a study of sixth graders, Koester (1961) found that their reading rate of science content was fairly rigid no matter what their purpose.

Smith (1967) used good and poor twelfth-grade readers to

study the procedures they utilize in reading for different purposes: getting details and general impression. She found that good readers varied their procedures widely, not only between getting details and obtaining a general impression but also within getting details and within the general impression. Poor readers used only a small number of different procedures when they read for both purposes. They were less able to describe the procedures that they used. She also learned that good readers were better able to choose an appropriate purpose for reading the experimental selection. However, neither group of readers showed much insight into the variety of purposes for reading that are possible in any one content area. "The better readers tried to place information in mind by several techniques, such as rereading, relating ideas, and reviewing the content. The poorer readers, on the other hand, tried to remember isolated facts and reread because they did not understand the selection." (p. 78) Smith concluded that both curriculum developers and teachers must pay more attention to explaining purposes for reading specific content and the variety of procedures that can be used to achieve that purpose. Teachers can use well-planned questions and followup assignments to help students with adjustments to purposeful reading.

These findings would suggest that the teacher needs to provide an explanation of how purpose can affect rate and then give students practice with various purposes for reading science to reinforce the concept.

Organizational structure

For several elementary school science texts examined by Smith (1963) there were identifiable organizational patterns for various selections. The patterns included classification, explanation of an involved process, instructions for an experiment, detailed statement-of-facts, descriptive problem-solving, and combinations of these. Though Smith did not attempt to measure which of those patterns occurred more frequently than others, it can be assumed that they are all of sufficient frequency to make it worth alerting the reader that he may encounter one of them in most of the science material that he reads. If he therefore sets himself ready to think like the scientist, or more exactly to think like the science writer, he will have a mental framework in which to organize his recall of facts and the main idea, and he will also have the beginning of a classification system with which to initiate a critical analysis.

In addition to preparation for specific organizational patterns, preparation for subject content can be provided by the classroom teacher. Some preliminary experiments with special organizational aids to prepare the reader to comprehend a selection have been conducted by Estes, Mills, and Barron (1969). The experimenters used three different kinds of material to prepare tenth-grade biology students for what they were going to read: one was an advance organizer paragraph in which the contents of the selection were previewed in statements of broad generality; a second was a structured overview diagram using terms from the article in a broad taxonomical perspective; and the third was a set of questions about specific facts and ideas in the selection. The latter was typical of the kind of questions reading teachers pose as part of a directed reading lesson, questions such as What is an electric circuit? Where does the power come from? When do you use different kinds of circuits? The results of this preliminary study showed no statistically significant difference between the advance organizer paragraph and the structured overview diagram, but it showed a statistically significant difference in favor of the structured overview over the purpose questions, and the structured overview over the group that had no introduction at all.

At this point, the apparent value in the research on these previewing techniques is that they give teachers some specific means for improving students' comprehension when reading science content, for all students using the tested preview techniques obtained higher comprehension scores than did those who had no introduction.

Typographical aids

In addition to the preliminary reading aids provided by the

classroom teacher, there are those available within the text it-self. Typographical aids are often provided to assist the reader in focusing on the important ideas, thus helping him to comprehend better and to retain what he has read. Christensen and Stordahl (1955) modified science selections to include one of six typographical aids: outline at the beginning of the selection, summary at the beginning, summary at the end, underlining of main points, headings in statement form, and headings in question form. No significant differences were observed between the effect of the six patterns of typographical aids upon immediate comprehension, delayed recall, and time needed in reading. This study provides evidence that the format alone will not assist the student in his reading problems. The teacher has to teach the student how to use the improved format, no matter what variation it may have.

Critical reading

The ultimate aim of all of this research on vocabulary, writing style, reading purpose, organizational structure, and typographical aids is to facilitate the comprehension of science reading materials.

It is the opinion of reading specialists that a knowledge and application of specialized reading skills will help students achieve better comprehension in their content subjects (Artley, 1959; Fay, 1965; Whipple, 1964). Their reasoning is that critical reading ability in content subjects is based on a knowledge of basic reading skills, including critical analysis, and on the special abilities that enable a critical analysis of a given subject. The responsibility for developing these critical reading skills cannot be assumed only by a reading teacher, then, for a critical analysis of a given content depends intimately on the application of critical reading-thinking skills to the specialized problems of that content. A transfer of training from reading under one set of conditions must be made to show the student how it applies under another set of conditions. For example, looking for the theme or point of a short story is akin to looking for the generalization in a science article; trying to relate events in a story to one's own life is akin to searching for application of the science generalization.

To better conceive where critical reading fits into the reading process and thus determine how to lead a student to read science critically, a reading-communication model can be used.

Ostensibly the science teacher can interpret what his students do when reading science only by what he sees. He sees them looking at the printed page, and then he sees or hears them give some response after looking at that page. However, guidelines concerning what takes place internally are available for teacher use. One of these is the reading-communication model represented in Figure 1 below. In a simplified way, the model portrays some of the major operations that promote the interaction between the printed message of the science writer and the person who reads it.

The reader decodes (relates the text to oral language), develops initial perceptions (sensory type meanings), generalizes to concepts, makes associations among concepts, assimilates the message (literally comprehends it), analyzes it, applies criteria in order to evaluate the message, and determines how to use (or not to use) what he discerns in the message. Critical reading is usually defined in terms of the analysis, evaluation, and utilization segments of the reading-communication model.

The reader is at liberty to stop the internal operations depicted in the model at any point. And it should be clear, too, that he may not be able to carry out some of the operations for reasons of inability or lack of instruction. Knowing that each of these stages is a possible stumbling block to the kind of critical reading that the science teacher desires from his students tells the teacher that he has to be prepared to assist his students with the competencies at the initial stages of the model as well as with those higher competencies of evaluation and application at the other end of the model. Specific examples of how to teach science content within the framework of the model occur under later headings of *vocabulary and word analysis, locational skills,* etc.

The science teacher should be interested in knowing that ef-

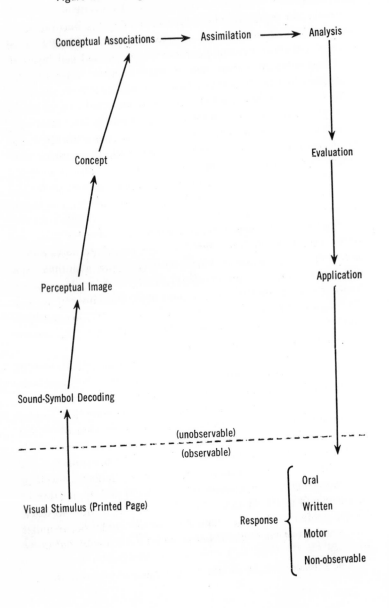

Figure 1: Reading communication process (A model)

forts on his part to teach his students how to read science critically may have significant payoff in their achievement in science content. It has been demonstrated through general achievement in content subjects that help in reading is correlated to significant advances in content achievement (Gilmary, 1967; Patterson, 1964). If it may be assumed that achievement on most standardized content subject tests is based primarily on literal comprehension, then the next step is to find evidence which indicates that the teaching of critical reading skills helps in a critical analysis of the content. In that regard, the evidence is not clear and the research is weak. Nonetheless, to get some indication of the factors that have been explored there is included here a brief mention of some of the studies related to critical reading.

A group of fifth-grade pupils benefited from exercises in creative problem solving. Even pupils with below-average IQ made significant advances in fluency of idea generation and in the ability to evaluate ideas in terms of the constraints of a given problem. The investigator recommended the development of long-term curricula which combine direct and explicit training of high-order thought processes like creative problem solving as part of a program for the improvement of reading skills (Covington, 1967).

Several investigators attempted to isolate critical reading factors from other comprehension factors without much success. They concluded that vocabulary measure is a distinct factor, but other skills in comprehension could not be separated from a common comprehension factor (Hunt, 1957; Maney, 1958; Sochor, 1958). Those conclusions, of course, may be altered as measurement specialists find more accurate ways of assessing the skills involved. There is some indication of the direction the measurement instruments may have to take in a study by Lundsteen and Michael (1966). They found that as the complexity of the verbal stimulus increased, the abstract cognitive style of thinking among third-grade children increased. Meehan (1970) suggested a similar phenomenon in regard to the kinds of questions asked of children. It seems that the children learn to identify where the payoff is in classroom tests and discussion questions. If most of the questions call for memory responses, they develop patterns of thinking that produce memory responses. On the other hand, if the question pattern shows reward for analysis and evaluation responses, after a period of time the children produce thinking patterns related to analysis and evaluation responses.

Clearly all of the previously cited research has important implications for future study. Reading typography and charts, analyzing text organization, using previewing techniques, engaging in problem-solving behaviors, applying criteria through evaluative operations: all are behaviors that need examining as they relate to reading science content. However, the present findings have current implications for the science content teacher who wishes also to teach relevant reading skills. Therefore, some specific teaching problems encountered by the science/reading teacher are discussed below.

Specific teaching problems

Vocabulary and word analysis skills

One of the particular characteristics of science vocabulary is the fact that science terms and their related concepts are not as likely to be in the experiential background of children as is, for example, the terminology of social science. A student may well read about the *federal judiciary* in the daily newspaper, but he will rarely find a term such as *landform* or *parameceum*. The teacher has the responsibility, therefore, of searching out ways to help the child visualize from his own experience what the new term is. Consider this single sentence: "Landforms are closely and intricately related to man's use and occupation of the land." The special word to be defined and studied for continued recognition is *landform*. However, the teacher may find it advisable to discuss *intricately* and *occupation* as well, remembering the research mentioned earlier which indicated that students often have more difficulty with the words surrounding the technical terms than with the technical terms themselves. *Intricately* and *occupation* simply may not be in the child's reading or understanding vocabulary. The teacher then works to establish and clarify the concept. Perhaps there are local examples which show that river valley land is used for grazing cattle and mountains for mining coal. By establishing these contacts with the children's experiences, the teacher enables them to understand the sentence, and probably the paragraphs that follow.

In some cases the science texts may be entirely too difficult for the students in the class or in a group. One way to cope with this difficulty is to find books which present the same basic content in a simpler fashion. Many publishers now produce supplementary materials with a less difficult vocabulary and concept load, for example, Holt, Rinehart and Winston's Adult Basic Education series. If these materials are written at a student's reading-ability level, word attack skills, context clues, and literal comprehension can be taught as the science concepts are taught.

Experience indicates that another major difficulty in science vocabulary is the fact that many words assume different technical meanings in different content. For example, *satellite* can be an orbiting celestial body, a country whose control comes from another "central" country, or a manmade object revolving around the earth. These possible meanings make it difficult to preview material and select at a glance the words that need concept development. Questioning the students about the material should provide information concerning their grasp of the meaning of a single word. However, such questioning should be carefully planned since repeating a statement from the book is not an indication of understanding. The question should draw out explanatory, definitional, or application responses. Restating may be relevant to a specific concept, for example, "What does *satellite* mean in that passage?" Application questions test the ability of the student to generalize the meaning and thereby illustrate his competence in dealing with specific content concepts.

A term in a book with an accompanying definition may not be sufficient for some students. The teacher may find it necessary to provide additional experiences with varying degrees of concreteness. For example, picture dictionaries, drawings, and manipulative models may be needed to bring about a concept such as "molecular structure," a term that appears in third- and fourth-grade science texts.

Locational skills

Locational skills refer to those skills needed to find information. The reader needs to know what kinds of information he can obtain from different types of books and reference guides. This area is especially important in light of the many materials these days that use an inquiry approach to learning science. Situations and problems are set up for the student to work out and to write the conclusion for. In a sense, the student then becomes one of the writers of the text; his job is to write the conclusion, the generalization, or the law that seems appropriate for the set of circumstances posed by the text writers. Thus he has to know the characteristics and the location of information sources such as textbooks, dictionaries, glossaries, science encyclopedias, trade books on science, tables of contents, indexes, science periodicals, and card catalogs.

Developmentally, a picture dictionary and its alphabetical arrangement are probably excellent starting points for building locational skills in the student. The teacher can have the class construct its own picture dictionary of the terms used in the science lessons. The concreteness of that task ought also to help with the concept development of many of the terms searched for.

But as the student's needs and abilities develop, other information sources must be utilized. A table of contents can be used to find the section where "molecular structure" is discussed or to preview a book to see if it will serve his needs. Glossaries, indexes, headings, pictures, and graphs can be explored as their use will serve the student in locating information that will help him with specific science content. It should be emphasized, however, that it is usually necessary to point out and explain each of these features to the student. He will not necessarily use them simply because they have been introduced in some other content or some other setting.

In the upper grades, formal instruction should cover the reference details required for meeting the more demanding informational needs. The teacher ought to call for locational skills frequently so that the students discover the usefulness of skills that enable them to find information quickly. Short exercises in using reference materials should be devised so that they can be completed in a 10-to-15 minute period. These exercises could include problems such as:

1] Given the topic of (life on Mars). What books does our library have on this topic? List their names and authors.

2] Select a topic from the chapter on reproduction. Using the index from four books, list the pages on which you would find information about this topic.

Short problems such as these can be checked individually, and as each student indicates his ability in the desired locational skill, he can be freed to explore a topic of interest.

Organization and evaluation skills

Ordinarily, a science teacher will expect a student to spend most of his reading effort in analysis and evaluation. The problem is—how can analysis and evaluation be taught, or more precisely, how is the student guided to learn them? A plausible answer seems to be to give the student demonstrations in the analysis of science writing and of the formulation of criteria to be used in evaluating the science material. In a sense, this comes near to asking the reader to think like the scientist, or more accurately, to think like the science writer, and it obligates the teacher to analyze a selection aloud for the benefit of the class and to develop criteria which the students can use to evaluate information in the same manner.

Besides an actual demonstration of what he means by analyzing and evaluating, one of the best tools the teacher has is his use of questions. But questions must be formulated carefully. It has been related in previous pages that students develop response patterns and thinking patterns in a given content as a kind of tracing of the types of questions asked repeatedly by the classroom teacher (Meehan, 1970). Thus the teacher who almost always asks questions demanding recall and nothing more will encourage students to approach that content with a mental attitude designed to recall but usually not to push the content further. It is evident that the science teacher wants an accurate recall of the content, but also something more. And what is important from the learner's view is that the learner should receive some concrete satisfaction for having pushed himself to do the analysis and evaluation that the teacher desires.

Students should be especially reinforced for responding well to questions that ask, How did the author organize the selection? How did the scientist organize the experiment? What weight of evidence led to the conclusion? What is the relevancy or utility of the selection? Those higher competencies related to the analysis and evaluation of a science selection can be summarized in this way:

1] Relate past knowledge and events to present knowledge.
2] Distinguish similarities and differences, fact from opinion.
3] Predict what the outcome of a series of events will be.
4] Draw conclusions or inferences from given data.
5] Reorganize the material to suit the purpose for reading.
6] Judge the relevancy, authenticity, and utility of the information.

None of these abilities is mutually exclusive, and they presuppose that the reader has the beginning competencies in reading on which he can base his analysis and evaluation.

Interest and style

Learning relies heavily on interest to get maximum benefits. Because most people are curious about the world and the way it works, there is a self-propelling energy that should be tapped by the teacher and by the text writer in order to carry the student into the subject matter. It is disturbing, then, to have research studies that report most science texts to be dull and uninteresting. Given that kind of situation, the teacher needs to consider means for making the reading material more interesting. Part of that job may simply be to make available a variety of books and periodicals so that all reading levels will have an opportunity to learn. The level of difficulty can in itself squelch interest. But more importantly, the teacher can provide films, filmstrips, manipulative devices, and paper visuals of all kinds to supplement the text and to spark the interest of the student.

Aids for science/reading classroom teachers

Almost invariably, teachers of science believe that the reading skills needed to comprehend science content should be taught by the reading teacher. This situation exists despite the considerations mentioned earlier, that is, that the relationship between the reading skills and the specialized science abilities is so intimate that they cannot be separated easily, and probably should not be separated except in the cases of those students who might be characterized as "remedial readers." The higher competencies of reading ought to be taught within a content (science) that is a valid concern of the student.

Yet assuming that everyone can be convinced of the importance of teaching relevant reading skills in the science classroom, the science teachers in today's schools usually are not prepared to teach the reading skills related to their field (Austin, 1961). Hopefully, the next generation of elementary and secondary teachers will acquire some of these skills as part of their education, but for the present most teachers either will have to gain these skills through inservice work or abandon the reading skills for science to an itinerant reading specialist.

Ideally, such an either-or choice should not exist. Regardless of the science teacher's competence in reading instruction, the reading specialist can serve as a resource person, as a very important teacher aid. The science teacher and the reading teacher can work together in analyzing the special characteristics of the science content that is being used. In that way, the science teacher can draw on the expertise of the reading teacher in designing exercises for identifying words, assimilating the message, or evaluating the material that is to be read.

Other teacher aids are also available, of course. There are two guides that might be very helpful to the science/reading teacher or to a team composed of science and reading teacher. One is a communication model which serves as a means of focusing on various facets of the reading act. The other is a cue sheet that lists some of the special problems related to reading science. With these two guides, the science/reading teacher or the reading and science teachers have a framework in which to operate and a list of specific questions or cues that can guide them in analyzing any science selection or book. For reference to the reading-communication model see Figure 1 and its related explanation.

Cue sheet

In addition to the broad concept of the communication model, a classroom teacher might find it quite helpful to draw up a list of cues that his students could use in approaching science reading. In fact, depending on the age and competency of the students, the cue sheet might be distributed to the class members. The sheet is not meant to act as a panacea but merely as a list of information that the reader of science material ought to keep in mind in order to read intelligently, that is, in order for intelligent communication to take place between him and the writer. A sample of the kind of cue sheet that the teacher and his students could use is found in Figure 2.

Figure 2: Sample cue sheet

Science cues

I. Vocabulary cues

A. There are certain words and related concepts that all pupils should know in order to read almost any science material above the primary level.

　1. An understanding of basic descriptive terminology such as *things in common, characteristics, various, classified,* and *similarities* is quite helpful in comprehending the data that follow the terms.

　2. Knowledge of common Latin or Greek roots or other derivations, e.g., *hydro, electro, photo, un, bi,* etc. facilitates understanding of new, but related, scientific vocabulary.

B. Every new science lesson requires the teaching of terms pertinent to that selection.

II. Typographical cues

A. Typographical cues are especially important in the first survey reading, because they offer brief but obvious identification of content.

B. Most science textbooks include typographical cues such as good subtitles, chapter headings, summaries, outlines, underlining or italicizing, indexes, glossaries, tables of contents, pictures, graphs, and charts.

III. Search cues

A. Certain procedures provide the general information sought from a preliminary survey of the material.

　1. Attention should be given to pictures.

　2. The organization of the content as it is reflected in the main headings and subheadings should be noted.

　3. The first paragraph and the summary, if given, should be read.

　4. Questions to be answered while reading should be formulated from the survey.

B. Other reading skills are needed to carefully search out specific information such as that required to answer the formulated questions.

　1. Careful attention to and analysis of facts and objective data are essential.

　2. Critical reading to determine the criteria for evaluating the content is necessary.

C. The ability to determine *exactly* what information is contained in the material is essential in reading science.

　1. A thorough discussion and evaluation of the reading is probably the best method to determine and insure accurate interpretation.

　2. Precision in reading is vital. Pupils should be urged to report exactly what they have read. For example, they must be aware of qualifying terms such as those identified in the following sentences:

　　a. *Most* kinds of bats are useful to mankind, because they eat harmful insects.

　　b. *Some* scientists believe there is life on Mars.

IV. Organizational cues

The most common organizational approaches used in science selections are deductive and inductive.

A. Deductive.
   1. Generalizations are given first.
   2. The subject is classified.
      a. General characteristics are given.
      b. Differences and similarities among the classes are noted.
   3. Examples and supporting data giving specific information about differences within the classes follow the classifications.
B. Inductive.
   1. The data are given first.
   2. Then the science writer builds up to classifying.
   3. Generalizations come last.

V. Special considerations

A. Science students must be able to read symbols, e.g., AuH_2O—gold-water.
B. They must be able to follow diagrams. For example, a student must understand the idea of completeness, as in an electrical circuit or a chemical equation. A diagram of an electric circuit when accompanied by explanatory text is an example of what the teacher can use to demonstrate that a diagram oftentimes can give a picture of the complete idea. The text then becomes more comprehensible.

Conclusion

Helping the learner visualize what the content is and helping him to have a purpose for reading rank high on the jobs of the science teacher, or more precisely, the science/reading teacher. Selective reading for a purpose is a dictum that applies to science content as well as to other content. Reading skills are not independent of the purposes for which the material is read, nor can those purposes be independent of the reading skills. The coordination of content with reading skills requires the identification of several factors:

1] The structure of the science content.
   A. What concepts does the author assume that the reader knows?
   B. What concepts does the author develop?
   C. What is the order of presentation?
   D. What style of presentation is used?
2] The purposes for which the material is to be read.
   A. What should the reader be able to do when he has read it?
   B. What concepts should he have before reading it?
   C. What concepts should he obtain?
   D. What is the reader expected to do with the material?
3] The skills of the reader.
   A. Can the student read the material and grasp the meaning and intent of the author?
   B. What reading and thinking skills should he have in order to read effectively and efficiently?

By answering these questions, the teacher can make decisions about what he has to do and what the student has to do to accomplish the objectives for the lesson in science.

In coping with science reading, then, the first problem is to identify the purposes of instruction. Next, the reading and thinking skills required to achieve those purposes must be identified. If the skills need direct instruction and practice in order to successfully attain the purpose, these skills should be taught in isolation so as not to interfere with the content form. If the skills can be taught simultaneously with the work in the science material, then that strategy should be used.

The availability of materials is not a problem anymore (though local funds may be). It is now a matter of the teacher's ability to bring content and child together by using some of the rubrics described in this paper.

References

Aldridge, B. G., and Anderson, K. E. Study of the relationship of fundamental skills measured by the National Merit Scholarship Qualifying Test to natural sciences reading ability. *School Science and Mathematics*, 1960, *60*, 439-44.

Artley, A. S. Critical reading in the content areas. *Elementary English*, 1959, *36*, 122-30.

Austin, Mary C., et al. *The torch lighters: tomorrow's teachers of reading.* Cambridge: Harvard University Press, 1961.

Blue, L. L. A study of the influence of certain factors in science materials on the reading comprehension of seventh grade pupils. Unpublished doctoral dissertation, Indiana University, 1964.

Christensen, C. M., and Stordahl, K. E. The effect of organizational aids on comprehension and retention. *Journal of Educational Psychology*, 1955, *46*, 65-74.

Covington, M. V. Some experimental evidence on teaching for creative understanding. *The Reading Teacher*, 1967, *20*, 390-96.

Crooks, K. B. M., and Smith, C. H. The reading problem in college science instruction. *Science Education*, 1957, *41*, 54-57.

Estes, T. H., Mills, D. C., and Barron, R. T. Three methods of introducing students to a reading-learning task in two content subjects. In H. L. Herber and P. L. Sanders (Eds.) *Research and reading in the content areas*, First year report. Syracuse: Syracuse University Reading and Language Arts Center, 1969, 40-48.

Fay, L. Reading study skills: math and science. *Reading and Inquiry*, 1965, *10*, 92-94.

Gilmary, Sister. Transfer effects of reading remediation to arithmetic computation when intelligence is controlled and all other school factors are eliminated. *Arithmetic Teacher*, 1967, *14*, 17-20.

Groff, P. J. Children's attitudes toward reading and their critical reading abilities in four content-type materials. *Journal of Educational Research*, 1962, *55*, 313-17.

Hill, W. Factors associated with comprehension deficiency of college readers. *Journal of Developmental Reading*, 1960, *3*, 84-93.

Hunt, L. C., Jr. Can we measure specific factors associated with reading comprehension? *Journal of Educational Research*, 1957, *51*, 161-72.

Kingston, A. J. (Ed.) Research for the classroom: content textbook—help or hindrance? By W. Hill. *Journal of Reading*, 1967, *10*, 408-13.

Koester, P. W. Reading science materials for two specific purposes at the sixth grade level. Unpublished doctoral dissertation, University of Illinois, 1961.

Lundsteen, Sara W., and Michael, W. B. Validation of three tests of cognitive style in verbalization for the third and sixth grades. *Educational and Psychological Measurement,* 1966, *26,* 449-61.

Maney, Ethel S. Literal and critical reading in science. *Journal of Experimental Education,* 1958, *27,* 57-64.

Meehan, Sister Trinita. The effects of instruction based on elements of critical reading upon the questioning patterns of preservice teachers. Unpublished doctoral dissertation, Indiana University, 1970.

Patterson, C. W. Pilot project in reading and study habits. *The Reading Teacher,* 1964, *17,* 531-35.

Severson, Eileen E. The teaching of reading—study skills in biology. *American Biology Teacher,* 1963, *25,* 203-04.

Smith, Helen K. The responses of good and poor readers when asked to read for different purposes. *Reading Research Quarterly,* 1967, *3,* 53-83.

Smith, Nila Banton. *Be a better reader.* New York: Prentice Hall, 1963.

Sochor, E. Elona. Literal and critical reading in social studies. *Journal of Experimental Education,* 1958, *27,* 49-56.

Stauffer, R. G. A vocabulary study comparing reading, arithmetic, health and science texts. *The Reading Teacher,* 1966, *20,* 141-47.

Whipple, Gertrude. Essential types of reading in the content fields. In J. Allen Figurel (Ed.), Improvement of reading through classroom practice. *Proceedings of the International Reading Association,* 1964, *9,* 31-32.

Williams, D. L. The effect of rewritten science textbook materials on the reading ability of sixth-grade pupils. Unpublished doctoral dissertation, University of Illinois, 1964.

Thomas H. Estes

Reading in the social studies: A review of research since 1950

This paper surveys research on reading in the social studies in the intermediate and secondary grades. The review of research is comprehensive in the sense that it includes the *significant* research published in reading since 1950. The small number of studies reviewed here reflects the state of research in reading in the social studies: a thorough search, made of research literature in preparation for the review, revealed how few scientific studies were actually carried out and how much more needs to be known before instruction in reading in the social studies classroom is to be fully effective. This is not to say that the insufficiency of knowledge prevents the teacher from proceeding, rather it is only to say that the present state of knowledge is at best tentative.

Three problem areas were singled out for attention in this review of research: 1] the reading skills necessary for achievement in the social studies, 2] strategies for teaching these skills, and, finally, 3] the readability problems that social studies texts present to students.

Reading skills and social studies achievement

The kind of skills necessary for mastery of the content of the social studies classroom is an important question in classroom practice. If a teacher is not aware of the reading skills needed for the mastery of content, he can scarcely be expected to teach that content. Research identifying reading skills necessary for achievement in the social studies has by no means been conclusive. Yet, research has provided some idea of the skill areas involved.

Krantz (1957), for instance, found that reading vocabulary and comprehension were related to social studies achievement. Krantz correlated subscores from the Iowa Tests of Basic Skills (a measure of reading achievement) of 471 seventh graders with the subscores of 256 of these same students at the ninth-grade level and 215 of them at the eleventh-grade level on the Iowa Tests of Educational Development (a measure of content area achievement). Not only were reading vocabulary and reading comprehension found to be the two best predictors of success in the social studies, but study skills such as map-reading; use of references; use of index; use of the dictionary; and reading graphs, charts, and tables were also found to be related to success in social studies. Thus, the Krantz study substantiated the contention that achievement in social studies is dependent upon reading skills.

It is not at all clear that the reading skills necessary for mastery of social studies can be isolated from each other. Goolsby (1966) found a high degree of interrelationship between reading maps, reading graphs and tables, using reference materials, judgment and critical thinking, knowledge of specific facts, and understanding of terms. The interrelations among these skills ranged from .74 to .99. Thus, Goolsby concluded that there is little justification for trying to differentiate between the skills needed for social studies achievement. Care must be exercised in interpreting Goolsby's results. For one thing, the fact that skills are highly related when tested does not necessarily mean that differentiating between them for instructional purposes is not useful or effective. Furthermore, correlations among tests such as the ones used here may be spuriously high. Two outcomes might appear highly related when the only thing they really have in common is that each is related to a third factor, such as to intelligence. Goolsby's study did not control for intelligence and, as a result, his findings are tentative. Even if Goolsby's results could be replicated with intelligence controlled and have the same results, it still would not indicate that it is harmful to *teach* specific study skills in the social studies class. Such results would say that there is difficulty in differentiating between specific skills by means of a test.

Correlational analysis has not been the only method for identifying reading skills important to social studies achievement. Melvin Michaels (1965) isolated skills on the basis of difficulties students reported they had reading American history texts. Students listed the following as areas in which they thought they needed instruction: 1] analytical comprehension (determining relative importance of facts and selecting main ideas); 2] finding sufficient information in references; 3] ability to summarize or generalize from facts; 4] readiness for reading (i.e., having sufficient background for the readings); 5] general comprehension and retention; and 6] retention of detail. In sum, these students reported difficulty in use of references, comprehension, and readiness. It is interesting to note that these students distinguished between analytical and general comprehension.

Sochor (1958) also distinguished between two types of comprehension, which she called literal and critical reading. Sochor administered a social studies, a reading, and an intelligence text to 513 fifth graders and found that the general reading test was not a good measure of either literal or critical reading in the social studies and that literal and critical reading are negligibly related to each other though each is related to intelligence. Therefore, Sochor concluded, training in literal reading of social studies materials does not presuppose or assure mastery of critical reading, or vice-versa.

While literal and critical (or analytical) reading comprehension, vocabulary, and specific study skills are important to social studies achievement, there is evidence to suggest that students are deficient in these skills at all levels. Robinson (1965) found that fourth graders were unable to employ reading skills necessary for reading in the social studies. In the Robinson study, 83 per cent of the students did not retain relevant details, although 75 per cent could locate details; 75 per cent could locate stated main ideas, but 58 per cent could not grasp unstated main ideas; 67 per cent did not compare ideas found in various sources; 58 per cent did not use tables of contents; 85 per cent did not use indexes. It is possible that students at the fourth-grade level had not yet had a chance to acquire these skills. But the situation is not much better at the upper-grade level as Perry's (1965) study with college students pointed out.

Perry asked entering freshmen to read a detailed thirty-page chapter taken from a history book in any manner they wished while bearing in mind that an easy quiz on the chapter would be given within two weeks. After 22 minutes, their reading was stopped and they were asked to report how they had been reading. More than ninety per cent reported that they had been reading the chapter straight through. All could answer questions about details but only one per cent could provide an overview of the chapter. The students did not apply study skills which might have been appropriate to the situation—skimming, looking for main ideas, establishing purpose for reading, etc. If college students do not yet apply or possess study skills appropriate to the social studies, it is unlikely that high school students do either.

From the research reviewed thus far, there is a basis for concluding that there are three basic reading skill areas necessary for social studies achievement: 1] vocabulary knowledge; 2] comprehension of both a literal and critical nature; and 3] study skills such as map reading; use of references; use of indexes and tables of contents; use of the dictionary; and reading graphs, charts, and tables. A limited amount of research further indicates that many students are deficient in all three areas.

Research on teaching strategies

Given that there are reading skills peculiar to the social studies as well as general reading skills necessary for achievement in the social studies and given that students do not have mastery over these skills, how can they be effectively taught?

There are two basic strategies for teaching these skills. One strategy has been labeled a "skills-centered approach." In it, the skills important to reading in the social studies are isolated and taught in special classes using whatever materials are available. Emphasis on content is secondary to emphasis on reading skills. Underlying this skills-centered approach is that skills learned in isolation readily transfer to situations where they are helpful in mastering content. A second strategy has been called "content-centered." In it, instruction in reading skills is integrated with the content of social studies. However, emphasis is on content rather than on skills; skills are taught only in a functional manner and only as they are required by the content.

The content-centered approach has received a great deal of attention in the 1960's. Proponents of it, such as Bamman (1963), Catterson (1965), Niles (1964), Smith (1965), and Strang (1966), have argued that the content teacher is as responsible for teaching the *process* of content acquisition as he is for actually affecting students' acquisition of that content. To teach skills separate from content and then expect transfer of those skills to functional settings, they have maintained, is unrealistic. Thus, they have advocated that reading skills be taught in the most functional manner possible as an integral part of the content.

There seems to have been no research carried out substantiating the relative effectiveness of these two basic approaches. Research instead has focused on the effect of teaching reading skills by using social studies materials, the "content-centered" approach. In general, this approach has been compared to an "approach" which consists of giving no instruction at all in reading skills.

Witt (1962), for instance, investigated the effect of teaching organization through outlining as well as drawing conclusions on social studies achievement. Two matched groups of 29 students received instruction for one semester by "usual" procedures, each receiving a different one of two units of content. During the second semester the content units were reversed and instruction in outlining and drawing conclusions was introduced.

At the end of each semester both groups were administered the Sequential Test of Educational Progress: Social Studies, the Iowa Silent Reading Test, and a teacher-constructed concept test. Greater gains were made on all measures during the second semester as compared to the first. For the social studies test and the concept test, the differences between the two semesters' gains were statistically significant. Therefore, Witt concluded that emphasis on these two reading-study skills was effective.

Fridian and Rosanna (1958) integrated instruction in reading rate and comprehension with the social studies content. Their method was simple: 24 reading selections of a summer session college history course were used as timed reading exercises with comprehension checks. Timed reading and answering questions following reading comprised the treatment. The students made gains in both comprehension and rate: average gain in rate was 194 per cent; in comprehension, it was 23 per cent. No control group was used and no statistical analyses were performed. The implications of the study, however, are intriguing—timing social studies reading and asking students to answer post-reading questions may enhance speed of reading, comprehension, and understanding of content. One should be cautious in applying this to the secondary or intermediate grade levels since college students have more highly refined skills and might respond better merely to being timed and asked questions.

Brownell (1958) investigated the effects of training in reading on the ability to think critically. The training in reading was given using social studies content as the vehicle for instruction. Unfortunately, Brownell failed to specify exactly what reading skills were emphasized. Two groups of 24 ninth graders received 28 weeks of instruction. For the group designated as the experimental group, this included two hours a week training in reading social studies content materials. The control group had no such training in reading. The study did not determine whether reading or social studies knowledge gain was greater for the experimental group. The Watson Glaser Critical Thinking Appraisal, however, was administered to both groups. The mean gain for those students receiving the training in reading was significantly greater than for those who did not receive the training.

Instruction in skills such as defining the problem; understanding key words; interpreting pictures, graphs, and legends; reading maps; and drawing conclusions has been found to improve students' reading of social studies materials (Hilsop, 1961). Schiller's (1963) investigation also demonstrated that achievement in social studies was greater after skill instruction. He emphasized five study skills: selection of references; use of index; map interpretation; dictionary usage; and the reading of graphs, charts, and tables. Subjects in the experiment were 288 seventh graders divided into five control groups and five experimental groups. The experimental groups practiced the skills during the process of acquiring information. Instruction in the control groups, while proceeding with the same content, provided no suggestions for using skills. Statistically significant gains were made by the experimental group on the Iowa Every-Pupil Test of Basic Skills and two tests of social studies achievement.

Zepp (1965) also found that instruction in basic reading study skills enhanced knowledge of the social studies content as well as reading skills. The basic skills Zepp taught were pronunciation skills, word meaning skills, basic locational skills, use of reference and nonreference books, and ability to locate materials in the library. Herber (1961) drew similar conclusions after a mid-year evaluation of an inprogress experiment with seventh graders. Herber's approach was to integrate skill instruction with the content. Vocabulary exercises were designed to provide practice in comprehension and study skills (unidentified). After five months, randomly selected pupils (every sixth one) took the Iowa Silent Reading Test. No control group as such was used. Gains of those tested exceeded gains made by similar pupils in past years in the same school district.

Several conclusions can be drawn from the research on teaching strategies. Instruction in reading skills through a content-centered approach has been shown to be effective in improving both general reading abilities and social studies achievement. However, in order to teach reading in the social studies class, skills necessary for achievement need to be identified and clarified. Finally, hard research is needed to determine if the skills-centered or the content-centered approach is more effective and further development of these approaches would be of value to the teacher.

Readability of social studies materials

Since some students are unable to read materials in the social studies, the teacher can help the student by adjusting the reading materials to suit the student. To do this, the teacher needs to be aware of the difficulties inherent in social studies material and the basis for assessing the readability of such materials.

One of the characteristics of social studies texts, as found by Arnsdorf (1963) and Wyatt and Ridgeway (1958), is that the range of difficulty within social studies texts is greater than the range of difficulty between texts intended for different grade levels. Arnsdorf, in applying the Spache Readability Formula and the Dale-Chall Formula to 25 books of four series in both primary and intermediate levels, found that while mean readability levels conformed to the grade levels on which they were used, readability within a text ranged on an average of 2.14 years. Wyatt and Ridgeway's findings were similar in their study of nine texts at the fifth-grade level. The average readability was appropriate for the fifth grade, but its range averaged 4.33 years within the text. Of the pupils surveyed, 14 per cent could not effectively read any part of their social studies text while 85 per cent had trouble reading some parts.

Since both the Wyatt and Ridgeway and the Arnsdorf studies were carried out on the elementary levels, their finding may or may not be applicable to secondary texts. This is not to say that there has been no research on the readability of secondary texts. Beard (1967), for instance, examined possible differences in stylistic variables between content texts in world history, American government, biology, and chemistry and how they might affect readability. Stylistic variables studied included sentence length, number of different words, percentage of complex sentences, number of infinitive phrases, and the like. Beard found no significant differences between the various content area texts, seemingly indicating that the type of reading skills needed in each content area may not differ greatly.

There has been some attempt to deal with the problem posed by the difficulty level of social studies texts. Arnsdorf (1962) modified textbook selections by replacing all indefinite terms, such as *high, many, years ago, low, large,* with definite terms. He presented the modification as well as the original to 412 students in the intermediate grades to measure their understanding. Answers to open-ended questions were scored. No differences were found to have resulted from the modification.

To date, there has been little research on how to overcome the problems presented by the difficulty level of materials except in terms of students, developing to the point that effective mastery of the content becomes possible. Research has provided procedures enabling the teacher to assess the appropriateness of reading materials for individual students. Bormuth (1963, 1967) developed the cloze procedure as a valid and reliable test of readability.

The cloze procedure, as explained by Culhane (1970), involves deleting every fifth word from a passage and replacing it with a blank space. Students are then asked to replace as many of the words as possible. A student who replaces 44 per cent or more of the words correctly should be able to handle the material with minimal assistance. Most of the research dealing with the reliability of the cloze test has been at the intermediate level and might not be applicable at higher levels.

In the late 1960's, research on readability research has been de-emphasized, because readability formulas have been found not to measure many factors contributing to the difficulty of content area reading. In fact, they assess difficulty by means of only two variables: sentence length and "familiarity" of vocabulary. Concept load is never measured by the formulas.

Future directions for research

As noted early in this paper, several reading skills have been identified as important to social studies achievement. These include comprehension, vocabulary, and a host of work-study skills. The crucial question in the area is not so much what or how many skills can be identified, but rather how reading instruction should proceed in the social studies class. What is needed now are studies comparing skills-centered with content-centered approaches to reading instruction. If research seems to indicate that the social studies teacher should devote part of instructional time to teaching the process of acquiring content, more attention should be focused on how that instruction is to proceed. Much of that research might center on the following questions:

1] Which reading skills are most crucial to social studies achievement? Do these skills vary across grade levels?

2] As skills instruction is integrated with content instruction in various ways, what is the effect on skills improvement and content knowledge? Are there other factors which might be affected by integrating skills instruction with social studies instruction?

3] What are the comparative merits of skills-centered versus content-centered instruction in social studies, especially when both content knowledge and reading skill are considered important?

4] What factors are crucial to the readability of social studies materials? How can social studies teachers deal with these factors? Are procedures such as the cloze technique applicable at levels higher than the intermediate grades?

5] What place is there for materials of a literary nature,

such as historical novels, in social studies and what would be the effect of their use?

6] Is there a place for commercialiy prepared reading skills training material specifically designed to improve content area reading skills in the social studies class?

References

Arnsdorf, V. E. The influence of indefinite terms of time and space on comprehension of social studies materials. In J. A. Figurel (Ed.), Challenge and experiment in reading. *Proceedings of the International Reading Association,* 1962, *7,* 159-61.

Arnsdorf, V. E. Readability of basal social studies materials. *The Reading Teacher,* 1963, *16,* 243-46.

Bamman, H. A. Developing reading competence through mathematics and science. In J. A. Figurel (Ed.), Reading as an intellectual activity. *Proceedings of the International Reading Association,* 1963, *8,* 110-12.

Beard, J. G. Comprehensibility of high school textbooks: association with content area. *Journal of Reading,* 1967, *11,* 229-34.

Bormuth, J. R. Cloze as a measure of readability. In J. A. Figurel (Ed.), Reading as an intellectual activity. *Proceedings of the International Reading Association,* 1963, *8,* 131-34.

Bormuth, J. R. Comparable cloze and multiple choice comprehension test scores. *Journal of Reading,* 1967, *10,* 291-99.

Brownell, J. A. The influence of training in reading in the social studies on the ability to think critically. *California Journal of Educational Research,* 1953, *4,* 28-31.

Catterson, J. H. Successful study skills programs. In H. L. Herber (Ed.), Developing study skills in secondary schools. *Perspectives in Reading No. 4,* International Reading Association, 1965, 156-69.

Christenson, C. M., and Stordahl, K. E. The effect of organizational aids on comprehension and retention. *Journal of Educational Psychology,* 1955, *46,* 65-74.

Culhane, J. W. Cloze procedures and comprehension. *The Reading Teacher,* 1970, *23,* 410-13.

Fay, L. How can we develop reading-study skills for the different curriculum areas? *The Reading Teacher,* 1953, *6* (6), 12-18.

Fridian, Sister M., and Rosanna, Sister M. A developmental reading experiment in a European history class. *Journal of Developmental Reading,* 1958, *1,* 3-7.

Goolsby, T. M. Differentiating between measures of different outcomes in the social studies. *Journal of Educational Measurement,* 1966, *3,* 219-22.

Herber, H. L. An experiment in teaching reading through social studies content. In J. A. Figurel (Ed.), Changing concepts of reading instruction. *Proceedings of the International Reading Association*, 1961, *6*, 122-24.

Hilsop, G. R. A study of division two social studies reading skills. *Alberta Journal of Educational Research*, 1961, *7*, 28-38.

Krantz, L. L. The relationship of reading abilities and basic skills of the elementary school to success in the interpretation of the content materials in the high school. *Journal of Experimental Education*, 1957, *26*, 97-114.

Michaels, M. L. Subject reading improvement: a neglected teaching responsibility. *Journal of Reading*, 1965, *9*, 16-20.

Niles, O. S. Developing basic comprehension skills. In J. K. Sherk (Ed.), *Speaking of reading.* Syracuse, New York: School of Education, Syracuse University, 1964. Pp. 62-74.

Perry, W. G. Students' use and misuse of reading skills: a report to a faculty. *Harvard Educational Review*, 1959, *29*, 193-200.

Robinson, H. A. Reading skills employed in solving social studies problems. *The Reading Teacher*, 1965, *19*, 263-69.

Russell, D. H. *Children learn to read.* Toronto: Ginn and Co., 1949.

Schiller, Sister M. P. The effects of functional use of certain skills in seventh grade social studies. *Journal of Educational Research*, 1963, *57*, 201-03.

Smith, Nila B. Reading in subject matter fields. *Educational Leadership*, 1965, *22*, 383-85.

Sochor, Elona E. Literal and critical reading in social studies. *Journal of Experimental Education*, 1958, *27*, 46-56.

Strang, R. M. Developing reading skills in content area. *High School Journal*, 1966, *49*, 301-06.

Wagner, L. D. Measuring the map-reading ability of sixth grade children. *Elementary School Journal*, 1953, *53*, 338-44.

Witt, Mary. A study of the effectiveness of certain techniques of reading instruction in developing the ability of junior high school students to conceptualize social studies content. *Journal of Educational Research*, 1962, *56*, 198-204.

Wyatt, Nita M., and Ridgeway, R. W. A study of the readability of selected social studies materials. *University of Kansas Bulletin of Education*, 1958, *12*, 100-05.

Zepp, G. D. The improvement of reading and reading-study skills in grades seven and eight through English, history, geography, and science. *University Microfilms* (Ann Arbor) *Dissertation Abstracts*, 1965, *26*, 218.

Test references

Iowa Every-Pupil Test of Basic Skills. H. F. Spitzer, E. Horn, M. McBroom, H. A. Greene, and E. F. Lindquist. Forms L and M, 1940 and 1941. New York: Houghton Mifflin, 1940, rev. 1947.

Iowa Silent Reading Tests: New Edition. H. A. Greene, and V. H. Kelley. Form AM. New York: Harcourt, Brace and World, 1933, rev. 1956.

Iowa Tests of Basic Skills. E. F. Lindquist and A. N. Hieronymus. Forms Q and R. New York: Houghton Mifflin, 1955-56.

Iowa Tests of Educational Development. E. F. Lindquist and L. S. Feldt. Form Y-2. Chicago: Science Research Associates, 1942, rev. 1963.

Sequential Test of Educational Progress: Social Studies. Cooperative Test Division. Form 3-A. Princeton, N. J.: Educational Testing Service, 1956, rev. 1963.

Watson Glaser Critical Thinking Appraisal. G. Watson and E. M. Glaser. Form YM. New York: Harcourt, Brace, and World, 1964.

Harold L. Herber

Reading in the social studies:
Implications for teaching and research

The previous paper reviews the research studies conducted since 1950 that investigate problems related to reading instruction in social studies. These studies are grouped according to three areas: 1] the reading skills necessary for achievement in the social studies; 2] strategies for teaching these skills; 3] the readability problems that social studies texts present to students. The purpose of this essay is to explore some implications for teaching and for research that can be drawn from the studies reported by Estes in the preceding paper. The content of this paper is divided into two sections: 1] teaching and 2] research.

The section on teaching is divided into four parts, each being a specific question: 1] Where should the skills be taught? 2] What skills should be taught? 3] What vehicle should be used for the instruction? 4] How can the skills be taught? These questions cut across the three areas presented in the preceding paper.

Teaching

A list of generalizations is given at the beginning of each part in this section. These are examined singly and in combination throughout the discussion of each part.

Where to teach the skills

1] Research suggests three ways in which teaching social

studies reading skills is related to teaching social studies content.

2] When deciding how to relate reading instruction to social studies content, logic and knowledge of principles of transfer must be relied on rather than research evidence.

Research suggests three ways in which reading instruction is related to social studies content.

Direct instruction in social studies class. This type of instruction starts from the premise that there are specific skills necessary for successful reading of social studies materials. A program of instruction is laid out, focusing on those specific skills. Social studies materials are gathered to serve as a vehicle for instruction. Time is set aside within the curriculum to teach these skills, the teacher departing from the content in order to teach them. This is due to the fact that the skills which are to be taught according to the planned sequence may or may not be appropriate to the assignments given in the required text for acquiring concepts being developed in the curriculum at that time. These would be skills of the type listed in the studies by Krantz (1957) and Goolsby (1966): map reading; use of references; use of index; use of the dictionary; and reading graphs, charts, and tables. The studies by Schiller (1963), Herber (1961), and Fridian and Rosanna (1958), apparently provided this type of instruction.

Reading instruction in reading class. This instruction is the same as the first type listed above, direct instruction, except for the location in which it is provided. The reading teacher focuses on specific sequences of skills. He uses the social studies material but not in reference to the development of the total curriculum or particular concepts within specific units. He gives direct emphasis to specific skills, using supplementary texts from the various disciplines. He may also make use of "content-type" material for the instruction. This type of material is available among the publications of Harper and Row, Prentice-Hall, or

Harcourt, Brace, and World Publishing Company for example. None of the studies reported by Estes in the previous paper seem to be of this type. That is, though some appeared to teach reading skills directly rather than functionally, this direct instruction was provided in social studies class rather than in reading class.

Skill-centered and content-centered approaches. In the previous essay, Estes refers to "skill-centered" and "content-centered" approaches to reading instruction. These labels have the same meaning as "direct" and "functional," respectively, and are useful classifications. However, they also should be qualified by reference to the location in which the instruction is given, that is, the social studies class or the reading class.

There is no clear evidence from the reported research to indicate that it is more effective to teach the reading of social studies in a social studies class—either directly or functionally —than in the reading class. No such comparative studies are reported by Estes. The research of Brownell (1953) and Schiller (1963) does suggest that direct and functional reading instruction in social studies class can improve students' achievement in reading and in knowledge of the social studies content. Moreover, all that is known about transfer suggests that the context in which the skills are taught should approximate as closely as possible the context in which the skills are to be used. To insure transfer from instruction to application, social studies reading skills should be taught in social studies classes. Thus, until research shows otherwise, schools concerned about students' social studies reading achievement would be well advised to establish an instructional program in which reading skills are taught in the social studies class.

Once a school has decided to establish such a program, there remains the problem of how to relate instruction in reading to the social studies curriculum. There is no clear evidence from the research to indicate an advantage in teaching reading functionally (content-centered) versus teaching reading directly (skills-centered) within social studies classes. Because no comparative studies have been conducted to indicate which course of action to take, teachers should consider two other factors when making a decision to follow either course: 1] economy and efficiency; 2] their total responsibility in training.

Logic indicates that the most efficient place to teach students how to read social studies material is in the social studies class. A sense of efficiency also suggests that the teaching of skills be functional (content-centered) rather than direct (skills-centered).

There seems to be a greater economy in the use of teacher time if reading instruction is functional (content-centered) rather than direct (skills-centered) within the social studies class. Treating reading separately from content—by teaching skills directly—has little place in an already crowded curriculum. Teaching reading so that skills are taught and developed in a functional manner within the social studies class consumes some instructional time otherwise devoted to covering the curriculum, but not nearly so much as when reading is taught directly.

A social studies teacher sees the teaching of the content of his curriculum as his principal responsibility. If reading skills related to social studies must be taught in a direct manner, the social studies teacher is less likely to devote time to this instruction when he feels that his time is already too limited to accomplish his prime objective. If instruction in social studies reading skills can be taught functionally, and if the teacher has developed the instructional techniques for this type of emphasis, he will then accept the responsibility of teaching both course content and related reading processes.

Few social studies teachers have received extensive training in the teaching of reading. When reading is taught directly (skills-centered) within the social studies class, it seems to require more specialized training on the part of teachers. As indicated earlier, the teaching might just as well take place in a reading class. The purposes would be almost identical since reading is taught for its own sake in both settings. On the other hand, if the reading instruction is integrated with the curriculum and the skills are taught in a functional manner, the teachers' training does not have to be as highly specialized. That is, it is not necessary that teachers be highly qualified in diagnosis and the treatment of students with reading deficiencies classified as remedial or corrective.

Thus, the reading skills necessary for mastery of social studies probably should be taught functionally (content-centered) in a social studies class rather than directly (skill-centered) in reading class or social studies class. This approach appears to be more economical and efficient. It realistically takes into account social studies teachers' responsibility and general training background.

What skills to teach

1] Research reflects a variation in points of view concerning the existence of a set of skills unique to the reading of social studies material.

2] Lists of skills identified as unique to the reading of social studies material have their origins more in authoritative opinions than in hard data.

3] Research suggests that instructional focus on broadly based cognitive processes (levels of comprehension, for example) is at least as effective as focus on narrowly conceived specific "skills" (locational skills such as use of index or table of contents, for example).

4] Apparent uniqueness of reading skills for social studies may, in fact, be the unique application of broadly based cognitive processes, appropriate (when adapted) to all disciplines.

Any discussion of what skills should be taught in a given subject area necessarily must involve an analysis of the basis for the view that separate skills exist for each subject area. This view has its origins in research conducted prior to the time restrictions set for the previous essay. Artley (1948), Shores (1943), and Fay (1950) examined the achievement of students as they read materials from different subject areas. They found inconsistent achievement across subjects. They concluded that different skills were required for different subject areas and that students did poorly in some areas because they lacked competence in skills unique to those areas. From their conclusions, and from conclusions of similar studies, there has developed the generally accepted view that although there are skills common to all subjects, each subject has a set of skills unique to itself.

These researchers could just as well have concluded that uniqueness did not lie in the skills required for performance in each area but in the adaptation of those skills—common to all subject areas—so as to meet the peculiarities of each discipline. The logic of this argument becomes apparent when one examines the following list of social studies reading skills (Bamman, Hogan, and Greene, 1961):

1] Vocabulary
   A. Technical terms
   B. Multisyllabic words
   C. Abstract words
   D. General terms
   E. Mathematical terms
   F. Concepts
2] Reading and deriving meaning from long and complex sentences
3] Reading important ideas and developing skill for retention of relevant events and developments
4] Locating and evaluating materials
   A. Gathering, organizing, and interpreting data
   B. Defining and analyzing
   C. Utilizing library facilities
   D. Reading maps, tables, graphs, charts, and formulas
5] Comprehending a sequence of events, simultaneous events and cause-effect relationships, (comparison-contrast relationships)
6] Discriminating between fact and opinion

7] Drawing conclusions and making sound inferences and generalizations

8] Speed

It is apparent that these skills could just as easily be applied to science, and most of them to literature and to mathematics as well. Though probably common to the four academic areas, these skills will have to be adapted to the peculiarities of each discipline as the skills are applied to different types of writing. Rather than learning separate and distinct skills, then, for each subject, students should learn how to adapt these skills to the peculiarities of each discipline. To some this may seem to be splitting hairs, but it is not. In this distinction lies the difference in orientation toward reading skill development: trying to find and teach skills supposedly unique to each area or teaching students how to make adaptations in skills common to all areas. The former view seems to lead naturally to the direct (skills-centered) approach. The latter leads toward the functional (content-centered) approach.

The labels applied to the skills identified as peculiar to various disciplines are also misleading. When examining the lists, the obvious conclusion is that uniqueness lies in labels (as well as in application) rather than in the actual process. The factor analytical study of comprehension by Davis (1968) tended to refute the existence of a multiplicity of discrete skills supposedly peculiar to different disciplines. Although Goolsby's (1966) study also tended to deny the existence of a multiplicity of discrete skills, Mr. Estes, in the companion to this essay, rightly points out that perhaps Goolsby's high correlations among the separate skills are spurious because each of the skills is highly correlated with the common factor of intelligence rather than highly correlated with each other. Estes infers, then, that these skills should be treated as separate entities and supports his view by referring to Sochor's (1958) study where she found, by factoring out intelligence, that literal and critical reading skills were not highly correlated. I believe that Mr. Estes' inferences should be modified somewhat.

There are discrete processes which should be given specific instructional attention. However, the research carried out by Davis (1968) and by Sochor (1958) suggested that these discrete processes are more broadly based than the extensive lists of skills in the literature would indicate.

Davis (1968) found the following discrete processes:

1] Recalling word meaning
2] Finding answers to questions answered explicitly or merely in paraphrase in the content
3] Weaving together ideas in the content
4] Drawing inferences from the content
5] Recognizing a writer's purpose, attitude, tone, and mood
6] Drawing inferences about the meaning of a word from context
7] Identifying a writer's techniques
8] Following the structure of a passage

Sochor (1958) identified two broad areas of comprehension which were discrete: literal reading and critical reading. Under these discrete processes many of the specific skills suggested in the literature as peculiar to social studies can be subsumed: those cited earlier (Bamman, Hogan, and Greene, 1961) and others. Of course, this categorizing is suspect since there is no concrete evidence that these suggested skills do, in fact, exist in isolation.

Implications for social studies teachers are clear. Rather than being concerned with these multiple skills suggested in the literature, teachers can devote their attention to the development of these broadly based, discrete processes. This action is consistent with the need to be concerned about the amount of time a social studies teacher has available to devote to skills instruction. It is more likely that he will spend the time if he can concentrate on broader processes in a functional manner, integrated with his curriculum, than if expected to teach multiple processes in a direct manner. Current thinking related to comprehension, and research into its application in content classes, suggests that emphasis on broader processes rather than specific skills is more profitable. Smith (1969) believes that the comprehension process is divided into four areas: literal, interpretive, critical, and creative. Herber (1970) suggests that there are three levels of comprehension: literal, interpretive, and applied.

Sanders (1970), Thelen (1970), and Herber (1964) demonstrate the efficiency of functional teaching of such broad processes within different disciplines. Sanders found a significant effect on the quality of students' responses to literature, specifically the short story. In Thelen's study, five months after being guided in responding to instructional films at three levels of comprehension, the experimental subjects retained significantly more knowledge of course content than the control groups. Herber found that students in physics, after instruction based on the application of these broader cognitive processes, scored significantly higher on the standardized content achievement test than did the control group.

Vehicles for teaching

1] The range of readability levels within a text is more suggestive of the potential difficulty in students' use of the text than is the average readability of the text.

2] Making texts generally more "readable" is not the solution to students' problems with social studies reading.

3] The extent and nature of teacher intervention is more important to students' success in reading social studies material than is control of vocabulary.

4] The organization of a text is no guarantee of students' success in reading it. Guidance provided by the intervention of teachers or by guide materials, or by both, is essential if students are to learn both process and content.

5] For those who believe social studies reading skills

should be taught functionally within the social studies class, the social studies text is the proper vehicle for skills instruction and practice.

6] There is a "seasoning" process that may take place in skill development. That is, one is able to apply skills or processes at increasingly sophisticated levels. This suggests that teachers should be more concerned about developing students' sophistication with these broader processes than with having students go through prescribed sequences among specific skills over a school year.

If reading instruction is to be taught functionally or directly in social studies classes, the only proper vehicle for that instruction is the resource material regularly assigned in the course. To use other vehicles that are designed especially to enhance reading skills is to separate reading instruction from the social studies curriculum. Naturally, then, the readability of texts becomes a major factor to consider when those texts are used as vehicles for skills instruction.

The complaint generally is that the texts are too difficult for the students for whom they are intended. Quite logically, teachers complain that it is difficult to give reading instruction through materials too difficult for students to handle.

However, the research on readability of social studies texts reviewed by Estes suggests that the problem is not as clear as might be expected. The true difficulty in the text is the range of readability, not the average readability. For that problem, there is a solution. A teacher can use the text for instructional purposes when specific selections, assigned for development of an understanding of content, are written at an appropriate level for his students. For other segments of the curriculum, other media for conveying information can be used if the text is too difficult. If sufficient emphasis is given to the development of these broader processes when students are reading segments of the book appropriate to their level, then they will gradually be able to handle increasingly more difficult segments of the text.

For example, students' responses to the text can be guided at different levels of comprehension: the literal, the interpretive, or the applied. Or, students may be guided to read with respect to organizational patterns: cause-effect, comparison-contrast, time-order, or simple listing.

This is not as neat a solution as might be hoped for, since the range of readability does not follow in ordered sequence from low to high from the beginning to the end of a text. Nevertheless, the procedure described still can be used since the broad processes of levels of comprehension and organizational patterns can be applied at a considerable range of sophistication.

There is a more important factor to consider than the readability of the vehicle: the intervention of the teacher. Durrell (1956) has suggested that teacher intervention directly, or through accompanying study guide materials, is probably a more important factor in students' success in reading than is the vocabulary level of the materials they are reading. Materials written "on grade level" can never substitute for an appropriate teacher intervention. Students must be shown *how* to develop skills. This instruction is of primary importance, and the appropriateness of the readability level of the material is of secondary importance.

Thus far, this paper has stressed the idea that social studies reading skills should be taught functionally in the social studies class. Further, the skills to be emphasized are broad areas of the comprehension process rather than the many, presumed, discrete skills identified in the literature such as those suggested by Bamman, Hogan, and Greene (1961) as given above. The vehicle, then, for the development of these more broadly based processes is the resource materials required in the curriculum, not special materials designed for separate practice of reading skills.

How to teach the skills

1] There is generally less research on how actually to

teach skills than there is on other factors contributing to students' achievement in reading.

2] Teacher intervention of some sort seems essential if students are to learn skills.

3] The real heart of the problem—how to teach students to read social studies material—is one of the most difficult problems to research.

4] Probably teachers should focus instruction on broad *areas* or processes such as "literal" and "critical," rather than on narrower, discrete *skills,* adjusting the levels of abstraction to suit the range of students up through the grades as well as within each grade.

5] Instruction should take the form of describing and showing, not just telling.

The paucity of research on methods of teaching reading as an integral part of the social studies curriculum is almost appalling. In fact, Herber and Early (1969) pointed out that this is rather characteristic of reading research in general and that approximately one-fourth only is directly focused on the issue of how to teach skills. The remaining three-quarters is devoted to matters peripheral to this central issue: matters such as readability, predicators of reading success, etc.

Nevertheless, some inferences with respect to techniques useful to social studies teachers can be drawn. Teacher intervention and guidance of students as they respond to the material are more important to success than is the control of the vocabulary in the materials being read. As Mr. Estes suggested in the previous paper, the organization of the text itself is no guarantee that students will succeed in responding to that text. It is necessary that teachers intervene and guide students so that they are aware of the aids available to them in the texts and that they know how to apply them satisfactorily.

Guiding students, through oral instruction and through written materials to accompany their texts, helps the students to develop a sense of the processes appropriate to acquiring an understanding of the content. For example, students may be guided as they read a required selection in their text so that they respond to it at the literal, the interpretive, and the applied levels of comprehension. Similarly, students may be guided to respond to the selection according to an appropriate organizational pattern: cause-effect, comparison-contrast, etc., the precise pattern to be determined by the organization of the specific selection being read. In either case, students perceive the content in the text and experience the process by which the content is perceived.

Although data are inconclusive at this point, they suggest that instruction of this type is effective for both students and teachers. Research previously mentioned by Sanders, Thelen, and Herber bear this out. On-going programs such as those described by Herber (1970) also support this view. Students learn process as they learn content; teachers teach process as they teach content. Reading is taught functionally, within the curriculum. Required resources are the vehicles for instruction. Students are shown how to read what they are required to read.

Research

The studies reviewed by Mr. Estes have implications for reading research as well as for reading instruction. He, in his summary, lists several research questions prompted by his review. These are focused on reading in the social studies. The research implications discussed in the remainder of this chapter are appropriate to reading instruction in all content areas as well as to reading instruction in reading classes. This discussion, admittedly, goes beyond the original assignment of drawing implications for teaching from the review of research. However, since the most unequivocal implication one can draw from the research is that some definitive research results are needed, the following discussion is most appropriate to this volume.

A general model is proposed here that takes into account two conditions that characterize research: 1] diversity and 2] comparability.

Diversity

Reading research efforts seem to fall into four categories, identifiable by type and location of reading instruction: 1] direct teaching of general reading skills in reading classes, 2] direct teaching of content-type reading skills in reading classes, 3] direct teaching of general reading skills in content classes, 4] direct or functional teaching of content-type reading skills in content classes. These types and locations are represented by four overlapping circles in Figure 1. An analysis of 180 studies reported in two reviews of research at the secondary level illustrates the range of concern (of lack of focus) in reading instruction. Sixty-three per cent of the studies fell into category 1; 6 per cent fell into category 2; 22 per cent fell into category 3; 9 per cent fell into category 4.

One of the strengths of reading research is its diversity of focus, involved in these four broad areas of concern. At the same time, however, this diversity is a source of weakness. Each of these areas is so broad that researchers seek new problems to study rather than refine findings from previous research.

Comparability

This urge for diversity and the search for new problems to research at the expense of refining promising solutions also prevents comparative studies that are sufficiently valid to warrant generalizable applications. If promising practices have not been refined through research to the point that they are reasonably predictable, then it is not possible to include them in comparative studies with other promising practices. The user cannot feel confident in applying the findings from a study comparing two procedures, neither of which has been refined to the point of predictable reliability. The extent of the failure to conduct reliable comparative studies is directly proportional to the

FIGURE 1

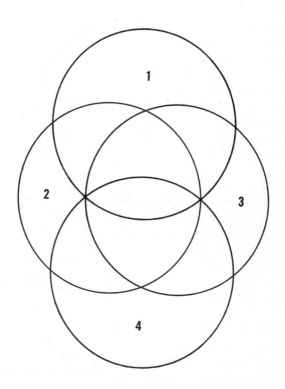

1. Direct teaching of general reading skills in reading class
2. Direct teaching of content-type reading skills in reading class
3. Direct teaching of general reading skills in content class
4. Direct or functional teaching of content-type reading skills in content class

FIGURE 2

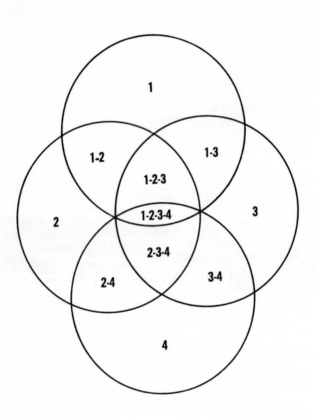

1. Direct teaching of general reading skills in reading class
2. Direct teaching of content-type reading skills in reading class.
3. Direct teaching of general reading skills in content class.
4. Direct or functional teaching of content-type reading skills in content class.

degree of preciseness of our knowledge about how to teach reading. That is, the more our research efforts are directed toward the refinement of procedures to the point of reliability, the more our comparative studies will have reliability. The more our comparative studies have reliability, the more precise we can be in our knowledge of what will work in given situations.

Long range model

A combination of iterative and comparative research is needed if the reading profession is ever to emerge from the present widespread research efforts with anything definitive to say about the teaching of reading. Krathwohl (1968) discussed an iterative study as one in which the researcher refines a promising procedure by adjusting variables within it, over a period of time and within experimental conditions, to the point that it is well defined and its results are reasonably predictable. Research energy should be directed toward iterative studies within each of the combinations of type and location of reading instruction symbolized in Figure 1, to identify promising practices in each. *Comparative studies* are needed within each of these areas of concern to determine the relative effectiveness of each procedure within each area. The last step, then, would be to run comparative studies among these four areas, as illustrated in Figure 2. Where the circles overlap in the figures, one can see possible comparative studies between and among areas. The most promising and well-defined procedures of Area 1 could be entered in a comparative study with well-defined procedures in Area 2. Similarly the other areas could be compared in various combinations: Areas 1-3, 2-4, etc.

Obviously, this kind of research would be a major undertaking, requiring intricate coordination and cooperation and massive funding. But perhaps its demands are no less realistic or attainable than the literacy goal for the 70's set for us by former Commissioner Allen (1970).

With such a coordinated research effort applied to such a magnificent goal, it might be possible by 1980 not only to speak with certainty as to what will and will not work with students but also to point to a literate populace as living proof of knowledge and practice.

References

Allen, J. E., Jr. The right to read—target for the 70's. *Journal of Reading*, 1969, *13*, 95.

Artley, A. S. General and specific factors in reading comprehension. *Journal of Experimental Education*, 1948, *45*, 181-88.

Brownell, J. A. The influence of training in reading in the social studies on the ability to think critically. *California Journal of Educational Research*, 1953, *4*, 28-31.

Bamman, H. A., Hogan, U., and Greene, C. E. *Reading instruction in the secondary schools.* New York: David McKay, 1961.

Davis, F. B. Research in comprehension in reading. *Reading Research Quarterly*, 1968, *3*, 499.

Durrell, D. D. *Improving reading instruction.* New York: Harcourt, Brace, and World, 1956.

Fay, L. C. The relationship between specific reading skills and selected areas of sixth grade achievement. *Journal of Educational Research*, 1950, *43*, 541-47.

Fridian, Sister M., and Rosanna, Sister M. A developmental reading experiment in a European history class. *Journal of Developmental Reading*, 1958, *1* (2), 3-7.

Goolsby, T. M. Differentiating between measures of different outcomes in the social studies. *Journal of Educational Measurements*, 1966, *3*, 219-22.

Herber, H. L. An experiment in teaching reading through social studies content. In J. A. Figurel (Ed.), Changing concepts of reading instruction. *Proceedings of the International Reading Association*, 1961, *6*, 122-24.

Herber, H. L. Teaching reading and physics simultaneously. In J. A. Figurel (Ed.), Improvement of reading through classroom practice. *Proceedings of the International Reading Association*, 1964, *9*, 84.

Herber, H. L., and Early, Margaret J. From research to practice: is there a time lag? *Journal of Reading*, 1969, *13*, 191.

Herber, H. L. *Teaching reading in content areas.* Englewood Cliffs, New Jersey: Prentice-Hall, 1970.

Krathwohl, D. An interview with. . . . *Journal of Reading*, 1968, *11*, 542.

Krantz, L. I. The relationship of reading abilities and basic skills of the elementary school to success in interpretation of the content materials in the high school. *Journal of Experimental Education*, 1957, *26*, 97-114.

Sanders, P. L. An investigation of the effects of instruction in the interpretation of literature on the responses of adolescents to selected short stories. Unpublished doctoral dissertation, Syracuse University, 1970.

Schiller, Sister Mary Philomene. The effects of functional use of certain skills in seventh grade social studies. *Journal of Educational Research,* 1963, *57,* 201-03.

Shores, J. H. Skills related to the ability to read history and science. *Journal of Educational Research,* 1943, *36,* 584-93.

Smith, Nila Banton. The many faces of reading comprehension. *The Reading Teacher,* 1969, *23,* 249.

Sochor, Elona E. Literal and critical reading in social studies. *Journal of Experimental Education,* 1958, *27,* 46-56.

Thelen, Judith N. Use of advance organizers and guide material in viewing science motion pictures in a ninth grade. Unpublished doctoral dissertation (addendum), Syracuse University, 1970.

Additional references

Herber, H. L., and Sanders, P. *Research in reading in the content areas: first year report.* Syracuse, New York: Syracuse University, Reading and Language Arts Center, 1969.

Herber, H. L. Reading in content areas: district develops its own personnel. *Journal of Reading,* 1970, *13,* 587.

Hilsop, G. R. A study of division two social studies reading skills. *Alberta Journal of Educational Research,* 1961, *7,* 28-38.

Smith, Nila Banton. *Reading instruction for today's children.* Englewood Cliffs, New Jersey: Prentice-Hall, 1963.

Zepp, G. D. The improvement of reading and reading-study skills in grades seven and eight through English, history, geography, and science. *University Microfilms* (Ann Arbor) *Dissertation Abstracts,* 1965, *26,* 218.

Joseph T. Brennan

The content directed experience and printed mass media: Their use in the content area classroom

The previous papers in this monograph have dealt with the reading skills necessary to success in a given content area. They each have been aimed at an audience with a given interest and with a specific need.

They each have offered much information of value to classroom teachers in these identified areas. The purpose of this final paper is to offer information and instructional suggestions that can be applied to any of these classrooms. The first section, the content directed experience, develops a step-by-step approach to classroom instruction centered around a basic text. The second section offers suggestions for selecting and using printed mass media as supplementary reading material in any content area classroom. Perhaps here the teacher will find some answers to the ever-present dilemma of how to match a student's reading ability to the difficulty of his reading materials.

The content directed experience

When reading teachers present a lesson from one of the basal reading programs to a group of youngsters, they have a general pattern of lesson development which the publisher suggests for use with his materials. Content teachers, because they frequently use a basic classroom text as the primary source of subject information, should also have a teaching procedure that incorporates many of the instructional practices of a developmental reading lesson. The exact method to be used may be adjusted by individual teachers in order to meet the needs of particular children; however, there are basic procedures which should be observed so that reading of content subject matter will be both meaningful and feasible for students.

Teacher preliminary activities

During this procedure the teacher previews the text material which will be read by the students. Particular attention is given to specialized vocabulary; concepts to be developed; author's writing style; special features such as tables, charts, maps, illustrations, diagrams, graphs; and any other reading skills that might need to be developed for a particular group of children. If these preliminary activities are to accomplish their ultimate purposes of stimulating interest in and facilitating understanding of the subject area, they must be pupil oriented. Therefore, the teacher must know the currently enrolled students well enough to make accurate appraisals of their needs and possible problems. The teacher should compile lists of this necessary information. (The lists will be used in a later step of the content directed experience.)

Introduction

Most content subject materials are grouped together into units which contain various concepts to be explored and understood by students in order to master the general theme of the different curricula offerings. Each new unit of study and each lesson within the unit needs a complete introduction if students are to realize maximum growth.

There are several principal activities which the teacher may initiate when introducing a new unit. During this procedure, every effort should be made to build upon existing pupil knowledge and interest. The new unit should be discussed in relation to other units which have previously been explored. Care should be taken to make the study of the new unit meaningful and relevant. Audiovisual aids, field trips, community resources, and student experiences are just a few of the methods which help to create student interest and involvement in the teaching-learning process.

Each lesson within a unit must also have an appropriate introduction. It is during these daily motivating periods that the lists of concepts, etc., which were developed during the teacher's preliminary activities are used. As was stated before, the teacher should know the various reading skills which will be needed by the students during each particular lesson and plan the presentation accordingly. During the lesson's preliminary discussion, as at all stages, student involvement is important and necessary. When concepts, vocabulary words, or any other necessary skills from the teacher's lists are offered during the discussion period they should be reinforced by use of 1] the chalkboard, 2] reference materials, 3] audiovisual materials, 4] word analysis skills, 5] demonstrations, and 6] any other explanatory means appropriate to the content subject. Having completed the preliminary discussion, the teacher will frequently have other necessary skills remaining on the compiled lists for a particular lesson. These are items which need to be introduced to students but which did not appear during the lesson's preliminary discussion. It is now necessary for the teacher to introduce the remaining skills before proceeding further with the lesson. Every effort should be made to make this somewhat isolated introduction as meaningful and as interesting as the preliminary discussion. These introductory activities will set the atmosphere for pupil development. It is here that the reading skills necessary for each particular lesson are developed. It must be understood that some students will need more of this preliminary instruction than others. This extra assistance may be given on an individual or small group basis while other class members proceed with succeeding steps of the content directed experience or as they participate in other related activities.

Previewing

Having completed the lesson's introduction, students should now be directed to the appropriate reading materials. During this previewing phase students should inspect 1] the titles of the various sections to be read, 2] the italicized and bold face headings and words, 3] the graphic aids presented in the material, 4] the form and style of the material, and 5] any other significant feature which may either give assistance during reading or pose problems for the reader. Each of these five previewing categories should be thoroughly discussed in class with as much student involvement and teacher explanation as is necessary.

When previewing, the teacher and the pupils should develop purposes for reading the content material. This may be done by formulating questions which the students hope to be able to answer during the reading of the particular assignment. These questions may come from section titles, pictures, graphic materials, student interests, or teacher-initiated ideas. But in all cases, it is important that these questions or purposes for reading be in the language of the students. As the student formulates questions, he will be setting purposes for reading the text material. By being in the student's own language, the questions will be quite clear for the student, and the reading of the assignment will be more meaningful as the student attempts to answer the questions which he has authored.

Reading and discussion

Students have now been well prepared for the reading of a particular text assignment. Many of the anticipated difficulties should no longer pose learning problems, and the individual doing the reading should now have the necessary skills and purposes which make the text assignment meaningful and attainable. Discussion involving students and teacher should follow the reading assignment. During the discussion students should seek to answer the questions which were formulated during the previewing phase of the lesson. The teacher may use this time to assist students with any difficulties encountered with the text materials and to appraise student understanding of developed concepts. It is important that this time does not become a mere question-and-answer period, with the teacher generating questions and the students reciting immediate-recall-type items from the text. The discussion should be a critical analysis of the materials read with emphasis placed upon meaning and understanding.

Independent activities

The textbook for any content subject is merely one source of stimulation for pupil development. No child should be restricted to a single source of academic exposure such as a basic textbook. During this independent activities phase of lesson development, the needs of individual students may be satisfied more fully. For some students the independent activities will be an extension of knowledge gained in the other phases of the lesson's development. Many of the students will have gained adequate understanding of the presented materials and will be enthusiastic to "go beyond" the regular lesson development of the text. These students will be engaged in a variety of independent and small group activities which will present them with an opportunity to practice and refine learned principles and concepts. The specific kinds of experiences will vary depending upon the particular content subject involved. It is here that each teacher must demonstrate content subject competence and provide pedagogical leadership.

For other students, the independent activities will be more of a re-teaching or further explanation and instruction phase of the lesson. These students may need to use materials which are written on a lower readability level or which further develop the lesson of the basic text. Teachers may also wish to use this time for more discussion with these students, particularly if the previous discussion phase of the lesson revealed a need for this type of supplementary instruction.

The suggestions contained in the content directed experience were designed to be used with a basic text as the primary source of student reading activities. However, it must be remembered that when possible students should be offered content subject materials from a variety of sources. Many of the research studies reported in other sections of this text have dramatically demonstrated the need for diversity of materials for all youngsters. The research has substantiated our professional judgments concerning the advisability of continually attempting to match materials to pupil skills, needs, and interests.

Reading skills relevant to all content areas

In addition to the procedures of the content directed experience described above, there are general reading skills which are relevant to the teaching of reading in all content areas. Among these are vocabulary development, reading rate, and comprehension.

Vocabulary. Content subjects contain an amalgamation of specialized terms which must be developed and understood if each student's potential is to be realized. For many students this is the most arduous obstacle inherent in the various academic areas. However, if students receive adequate vocabulary development in class and are provided with sufficient reinforcement through listening, speaking, reading, and writing, the technical language will develop as an aid to understanding and not merely as a cumbersome divergent to learning. Each content area teacher must assume the responsibility of developing the vocabulary peculiar to his curriculum, because it is within the various content classes that specialized language can be developed and practiced most successfully. Teachers must encourage students to use the specialized language of the subject rather than to avoid it.

Reading rate. Improving the rate, or speed, at which students read content subject materials is an important consideration, but it is not an ultimate goal of content classroom instruction. Specific remedial or developmental instruction in reading rate is primarily the responsibility of the reading teacher. The responsibility of the content classroom teacher is to guide the student in applying the skills he has learned by helping him adjust his reading speed to his specific content area comprehension needs. He must achieve a balance between speed and comprehension. The content area teacher should encourage him to evaluate his reading speed and to make adjustments when necessary, but these adjustments should be initiated only for the purpose of producing maximum speed and maximum understanding. Generally, both reading speed and comprehension are dependent upon 1] the purpose of the reader, 2] the skill of the reader, and 3] the difficulty of the materials to be read. In the content subjects, a student's reading purposes will vary depending upon the phase of the lesson in which the student is involved. At times the student will be reading for initial information, and his speed will be slower than at other times. Later, he may be reading from supplementary sources about already understood concepts and his speed will be significantly faster. However, any reader's skill is an important determiner of his speed. A student who manifests appropriate skills in vocabulary, word attack, and comprehension should be encouraged to increase his reading rate to maximum productivity. If a student does not demonstrate adequate development in these three basic skill areas, relatively little emphasis should be placed on reading speed until the areas are developed. All students should be led to realize that reading speeds must be individually determined levels. Every effort should be made to increase their reading speeds so long as understanding is not sacrificed.

This understanding is, of course, directly related to the difficulty of the material being read, and the difficulty of the material must be determined by each student individually. Material which is difficult for one student may be relatively easy for another. The more difficult the material is for an individual, the slower it must be read in order to be understood. When discussing speed, content area teachers should inform students that merely reducing speed will not increase comprehension if the material being read is too difficult for their level of reading ability. If this is the case, a more appropriate reading material must be sought.

Comprehension. Comprehension of written materials must be an important goal in any content area classroom. All of the activities of the content directed experience were designed to produce improved comprehension and to make subject areas interesting for the students. Yet each content area may develop additional activities which aid in producing better understanding for its students. Some general activities which content teachers may use to develop comprehension are the following:

1] Outlining—In this activity, students must identify main ideas and supporting details. It is important that they receive instruction in a simple outlining procedure and that they not be restricted by the structured mechanics of the process. The purpose of this type of outlining is to identify ideas rather than to produce a finished product, and it may be done either as an independent activity or as a group or class activity during the discussion phase of the lesson.

2] Reading for details—This may be accomplished by formulating specific purposes for reading so that students will be reading to investigate specific, predetermined aspects of the materials. However, content classroom teachers who use this activity must be careful that students do not omit important items of information as the result of their search for specific details. If this activity is undertaken, teachers must use the developed understandings as a nucleus for other lessons. No subject area teacher should be satisfied with students who possess an accumulation of specific facts; understanding, appreciation, and utilization of the content subject must be the ultimate objective.

3] Summarizing—Having read the text material and appropriate supplementary materials, students may summarize the understandings attained. This activity will help the students to preserve the essential aspects of the lesson and will serve as an excellent source for systematic review.

4] Writing questions—Students may formulate questions either before or after reading the content materials. These questions should then be answered in the student's own words and when possible should be shared with other classmates.

These are just a few of the general activities which will help to promote comprehension of content subjects. These activities, and many others, should be adapted to the particular academic offering so that student development may be realized to individual potential.

Printed mass media

Research in the various content areas has indicated that textbooks often are not suitable to the reading levels of the students who are to use them, nor are they always the most appealing reading matter to these students. In fact, the books' outward appearance alone often discourages the prospective reader. Therefore, in an effort to solve these problems, teachers in all content areas are using more supplementary reading materials. One of their major materials sources has proved to be the printed mass media. Newspapers and magazines offer the students and the teachers the type of flexibility they are seeking in the areas of interest, readability, and format. These materials are readily available, and they are "up-to-date." In short, they are a timely and versatile text.

Because this situation exists, a section on the use of printed mass media in the classroom seems a useful companion to a section proposing a content directed experience which can be adapted to various content classrooms. This media section will deal specifically with the ideas that 1] certain criteria must be used in selecting media that appeal to and can be understood by children; 2] certain skills are necessary for effective newspaper reading; and 3] these skills are related to specific content areas and can be taught in these classrooms.

Readability

As is obvious, if a teacher is to avoid sustaining the problem of offering the student inappropriate and/or unappealing reading matter, consideration must be given to selecting newspapers and magazines that can be read and enjoyed. Research has shown that the following variables affect the readability of printed mass media: format, length of item, type of reporting, level of reading difficulty, and content. Particular attention should be given to each of these before a final selection for classroom use is made.

Format. Perhaps initial consideration should be given to format, since the student becomes aware of that aspect of the newspaper or magazine first. He is immediately conscious of any visual stimuli included in the format, and he tends to focus his attention on the items to which they relate. Swanson (1955), studying 130 United States daily newspapers from 1939 to 1950, found that cartoons, photographs, and photograph outlines showed a higher degree of readership than any other newspaper feature. He also found that graphs, tables, and texts enhanced understanding of news stories based primarily on statistics. Among the latter three forms of visual stimuli, Wilcox (1964) found the bar graph to be most effective. Thus, visual stimuli serve not only to attract student readers but also to aid them in their reading. These findings suggest that newspapers which emphasize visual stimuli will be both more appealing to and more easily understood by most students.

An additional type of visual stimulus which immediately attracts a reader's attention is the printed headline. While it is similar to a photograph or cartoon in function, it demands additional reading skills. Its letters must be deciphered before it can be comprehended. Once comprehended, the headline must indicate to the reader an article's content and arouse his interest in reading further. Obviously some newspapers accomplish this more successfully than others.

Haskins (1966), using 12 newspapers, tested the accuracy of news classification on the basis of headline and headline-and-lead reading. He found this scanning method to be 76 per cent accurate for identifying the rather obvious category of foreign news items. Within this category, identification of foreign affairs items dealing with the United Nations proved 83 per cent accurate. However, for the various newspapers studied, there was a 64 to 84 per cent variation in the accuracy. This means that headline scanning is more effective for some newspapers than for others.

One reason for lack of recognition and comprehension of headlines seems to be the substitution of initials for words in order to achieve brevity. Goldsmith (1958) studied headlines which contained initials judged to be in general use, yet not as well known as the words or phrases they represented. His subjects evinced a mean knowledge of 63 per cent of the initials alone, but they recognized only 60 per cent of them when they appeared in the selected headlines. The researcher concluded that headline writers are overestimating the ability of readers to understand headline initials and that context does little to aid in comprehension. If such a situation is true of adults, the problem can easily be compounded for junior high students possessing less general knowledge of world affairs. Therefore, special attention should be paid to how easily headlines will be understood by children using printed mass media as a supplementary classroom material.

Another element of format to be considered in newspaper selection is item placement. Location influences what items will or will not be brought to the attention of a reader. Schramm and Ludwig (1951) reported that items on page one of a newspaper are about twice as likely to be read as items on any other page. Stern (1951) determined front-page mean readership to be 194.3 as compared to 148.3 for the first page of the second section—another favorable location for item placement. Right-hand pages are more likely to be read than left-hand pages (Schramm and Ludwig, 1951). Baker and MacDonald (1961) concluded that editorials occupying the lead position on the editorial page obtain better readership than those in other page locations. Given these findings, some check of the placement of types of articles to be emphasized in a content classroom would seem warranted.

Item length. A readability variable, closely related to format, which influences a person's reading selection is article length. It is interesting to note that two researchers found that long articles and editorials often attract more readers than short ones. Ellison and Gosser (1959) reported that readers of nine magazines were attracted to long, nonfiction articles that interested them. Baker and MacDonald (1961) found that long newspaper editorials had a higher readership rate than short ones. Thus, it would seem that some students will want an opportunity to read longer articles than are regularly provided in mass media printed especially for classroom use.

Type of reporting. However, the fact that a student may notice and read an item, either long or short, does not guarantee that he will understand it. This is especially true in the case of news items. Often the facts alone are not enough to clearly explain a point; some interpretation is necessary. Griffin (1949) and Sennett (1954) have demonstrated the need for interpretative reporting. Griffin found that less than half of the readers of a San Francisco paper had sufficiently accurate comprehension of news items to report the content detail. Sennett determined that interpretative reporting was significantly more effective for comprehension than the regular "straight-forward" news reporting. In this latter study, the subjects who read interpretative stories answered twice as many interpretation questions correctly as those who read items in the regular reporting-style text. Such an aid to comprehension would seem especially important for unsophisticated readers.

Material difficulty. Yet even the best interpretative reporting cannot compensate for reading material which is too difficult for a student's level of reading achievement. Special care must be taken to select supplementary printed media that provide enough readability range to meet the needs of the various students who will be using them. Research done by Anderson (1966), Danielson and Bryan (1964), and Stevenson (1964) gives some idea of the readability level which can be expected in various types of newspapers and news items. However, to be certain of the readability level of a particular newspaper or magazine under consideration for supplementary material, a check using a readability formula would seem wise.

Anderson (1966) found the reading difficulty of 14 Australian newspapers to range from seventh- or eighth-grade levels to high school and university levels. In a similar study, he found that the reading difficulty of the *Cumberland Evening Times* ranged from fifth- and sixth-grade levels for human interest stories to grades thirteen and fifteen for editorial items. Danielson and Bryan (1964) found a mean readability of seventh grade for hard news items and 6.4 for soft news items received from the North Carolina Associated Press Teletypesetter Wire.

Stevenson (1964) studied changes in the readability of conservative newspapers (those which stressed responsibility and concern for mature journalism) as compared to those in sensational newspapers (those which attempted to attract lower socioeconomic readers through stories having emotional appeal). Results indicated that conservative newspaper readability had not increased significantly since 1872. However, the reader of a sensational newspaper would find it easier to read today than at this earlier date.

Content. As is obvious, content is a major factor which influences the readability of sensational newspapers. It is generally a major influence in any printed news media and should be considered in selecting classroom materials. Perhaps the first content-related considerations should be those of content source and content type. Most newspaper content is obtained from the various wire services which distribute news to the entire United States, and a study by Gold and Simmons (1965) has shown little variation among 24 Iowa daily newspapers in the relative frequency of the types of stories used in relation to the total amount of news items used. In general, the newspapers which printed larger proportions of any category of news stories were those papers which printed larger proportions of the total amount of wire service stories. There was no evidence that a greater use of wire stories by a newspaper represented different decisions about the types of stories to emphasize. The newspapers which used a greater number of wire stories apparently printed the same stories as the papers which used a similar percentage, plus additional stories in each subject area. Thus the relative distribution of subject matter was unaffected.

The actuality of similar news coverage was supported by Deutschmann (1959) who studied seven New York, three Cleveland, and two Cincinnati newspapers. He found a commonness correlation of .86 among these papers in terms of their coverage of news items and editorial materials. Stempel (1962) found that although coverage is similar, small town dailies place more emphasis on hard news items than do large daily newspapers. Since these studies demonstrate that most newspapers obtain much of their content from the same sources and provide similar news items, the selection criterion becomes primarily one of quantity of material rather than type. Therefore, the teacher might do well to consider the idea of making a student better informed on a subject by providing him with as much relevant material as possible.

However, quantity alone is not a sufficient basis for selection. The influence a newspaper's content can have on its readers and the accuracy of that content must also be considered before a final selection is made. It is a generally accepted truth that what a person reads has some influence on him. Edelstein and Larsen (1960) demonstrated evidence of a newspaper's sociological influence, and Brinton and McKown (1961) demonstrated its educational influence. The former researchers found that the most frequent readers of weekly community newspapers demonstrated the highest degree of community feeling. They concluded that the newspaper served as an instrument to integrate both individuals and groups into the community structure. Brinton and McKown found that newspaper readers in two adjoining communities (only one of which had to decide upon the installation of a water fluoridation system) showed 1] greater knowledge of fluoridation and 2] a firmer opinion on the subject than did nonreaders, because both communities received exposure to the topic through their local newspaper.

Yet a publication's influence may not always be good.

Teachers should carefully analyze the accuracy of printed news media's content both in terms of factual information and subtly presented bias or prejudice. Factual information can easily be evaluated through cross-checking the same news item in several media, but propaganda is more difficult to identify. It often appears in the form of an excessively favorable and appealing description of a given subject. For example, Dasbach (1966) found that neither *America Illustrated* nor *Soviet Life* overtly categorized the other nation as bad or weak. Rather they concentrated on building a good self-image.

Another common propaganda device of which a teacher must be aware is the use of ambiguous statements which encourge a reader's own prejudices. Engel, O'Shea, and Mendenhall (1958) found that their subjects interpreted mass media ambiguities in terms of their personal biases.

Readership

To this point in the paper, emphasis has been placed on the importance of format and content as criteria for selecting printed mass media for classroom use. But these are only part of the criteria which should be considered. As was stated earlier, the fact that a material's reading difficulty and content are suitable to a student's ability does not guarantee that it will be a successful teaching device. It must also appeal to the prospective reader. In order to select such materials, a teacher must have some knowledge of students' reading habits and interests as they relate to printed mass media, be willing to accept these existing interests and develop them into broader areas—especially in terms of information relevant to a given content area, and be aware of the effect of maturation on reading material preferences.

Care must be taken to select materials that range from those written especially for young people to those written for adults. Although providing materials that are too sophisticated and difficult can create problems, the contrary is equally ill-advised. Students must not be insulted by materials that they have "outgrown." For example, Stewart (1964) found that adult mag-

azines showed a higher degree of popularity among young readers than did teen magazines. Seventh and eighth grades were
peak teen-magazine reading years for boys, and even then most
boys considered them "trash." Girls' interests declined steadily
from the seventh through the twelfth grades.

However, factors other than age affect students' reading
tastes. Their preferences for particular sections of the newspaper often vary according to their interests and abilities. Results
of a study by Lyle (1962) indicated that sixth and tenth graders
who read hard news items were more interested in attending
college than were those who read the entertainment sections.

Yet certain general conclusions regarding interest can be
drawn. A study by Johnson (1963)[1] indicated that 504 fourth,
fifth, and sixth graders preferred the comics to all other sections
of the newspaper. Their second preference was front page
news; third was sports news.

Also research has shown that, regardless of his age, local
news stimulates a reader's interest. Personal involvement provides a reason for reading. In a study of 41 newspapers, Stern
(1951) found that pages containing local news (regardless of
their location) were well read. Other research indicated that a
weekly community paper received its highest readership when
community news held the dominant news-frequency position
and that the percentage of items read varied inversely with the
circulation of the paper (Schramm and Ludwig, 1951; Carter
and Clarke, 1963). These latter findings suggest that community size is directly related to a reader's interest in local news;
as the community served by a newspaper becomes larger, the
news items lose their local identification for the reader. Therefore, a teacher planning to use local newspapers primarily as a
means of attracting student interest in supplementary reading
materials should consider the degree of personal involvement
that will be stimulated by the chosen media.

Hopefully, the above information will provide some guide-

---

[1]This study, although conducted at the elementary level, is included because of
lack of appropriate secondary-level studies. Its findings seem relevant to both levels.

lines for capitalizing upon students' reading interests and preferences as a means of enticing reluctant readers to read in any content area. An interest in comics which is properly encouraged can develop into content-related qualities such as an appreciation for satire, an interest in history, or an awareness of social problems.

Skills necessary for effective newspaper reading

When newspapers are used as supplementary reading materials, content area teachers must be responsible for instructing students in the reading skills necessary for effective utilization. In doing this, they must be especially careful not to assume too much prior knowledge on the part of their students. Research has shown that often students are not familiar with even the most general information concerning newspapers. Gregory and McLaughlin (1951) found that only six of their 27 junior high students knew something of the purposes and functions of the editorial page; none thoroughly understood the terms *lead, columnist, Associated Press, United Press,* or *syndicates.* These findings suggest that the general skills of 1] identifying the location and content of particular newspaper sections and 2] explaining specific terminology used to describe the newspaper must be taught in some classroom. Obviously, however, there is no need for repetition in each classroom. Perhaps these general skills can be explained most effectively by the school's reading or English department because the study of the newspaper and other forms of written mass media is generally a segment of their curricula offering.

Once these skills are taught, emphasis can be placed on the skills necessary for reading content-related newspaper sections in particular classrooms. Because different content subjects will use different newspaper offerings, this specific instruction becomes the responsibility of each content classroom teacher.

Some content-related skills overlap into each classroom with only a change of content or emphasis. For example, each classroom teacher should be aware of the initials currently being used in news stories dealing with his particular content area so that he can clarify for his students any confusion with headlines or articles incorporating such abbreviations. Also, several teachers might have students follow a series of articles on a content-related subject over an extended period of time in order to observe differences in reporting, to analyze news offerings, and to understand the sequence of events. Some discussion of the type of bias or prejudice likely to occur in the reporting of content-related articles should also take place in each classroom.

Many skills, however, apply more specifically to one content area than to others.[2] For example, literature classes would probably read the book, theatre, and movie reviews. They would read news items about authors and/or about topics related to study units such as individual freedom, the generation gap, and the battle of the sexes. They might also study comic strips, syndicated columns such as Art Buchwald's, and political cartoons as media of satire, or they might read human interest stories, editorials, and letters to the editor as examples of various writing styles, author bias, or different presentation approaches to similar material. These selections require a knowledge of specialized vocabulary and specific critical reading skills which should be taught before the material can be effectively used.

Various social studies classes would obviously emphasize selections such as international and local news, political cartoons, and syndicated political columns such as William Buckley's. They might also read editorials and even advertisements in their search for propaganda techniques. Ultimately they might study the entire newspaper as a record of political and social history. Once again specialized vocabulary and critical reading skills are important.

In addition to science-related news stories such as those reporting space exploration, science classes might regularly read syndicated columns on medicine and/or gardening, comic strips

[2]A description of each subject area's particular newspaper-reading skills would be too lengthy and involved for this general discussion. Hopefully, the examples given will offer direction for any classroom teacher. Specific instruction for teaching many of the skills discussed are given in the relevant sections of the preceding papers.

such as *Rex Morgan* or *Dick Tracy,* and the weather map. Specialized vocabulary and symbols, map-reading skills, and methods of organizing and presenting specific factual information must be taught before the material can be effectively used.

Finally, math classes might read the statistics in the sports section, the grocery ads, the classified ads, the TV schedule, and mathematics-related news stories such as the change in the English monetary system. Checking batting averages or team ratings, figuring unit prices for advertised products, comparing prices of similar products, and computing monthly, weekly, or hourly wages for certain jobs provide exercises in setting up and solving practical mathematics problems. Reading the TV schedule offers a young child practice in time computation as well as in reading a table. Each of these activities requires advance preparation for the student by the teacher.

Concerned content area teachers who see that their students are familiar with the total newspaper as well as with the specific sections that apply to the different subject areas develop in their students a reading ability which transcends the classroom. These students will have discovered a valuable information source which is available to them at any time in their lives, and, perhaps more important, they will have learned to use it effectively.

Adding this long-range goal to the more immediate one of supplementing standard classroom texts gives even more impetus to the careful selection of printed mass media for classroom use, to the utilization of student interests in developing a supplementary reading program, and to providing students with the skills necessary to effectively use these media both in and out of the content classroom.

Conclusion

One purpose of this paper was to present content area teachers with instructional procedures designed to assist students in the reading activities of various subjects. A second purpose was to report research conducted with printed mass media and to suggest instructional implications for content teachers as they use various types of these media. The content directed experience was explained in considerable detail and should be used when textbooks and other printed material are to be read by students. The investigations analyzing the usage of newspapers and magazines overlap into many content areas but were treated separately for the purpose of reporting and relating completed research which has been authored by many individuals, some of whom are educators and some noneducators.

The challenge of teaching reading to the students in our schools must be accepted by every teacher. To many students it is not so much the subject matter that is the primary source of academic frustration as it is their undeveloped reading potential. All teachers, reading specialists and content teachers alike, must be perceptive to the reading needs of students. Children must continually receive general reading instruction, and they must also be instructed in the specific skills which are needed in each content subject. Developmental reading classes can do much for developing the general reading skills of children. However, the content subject classes are the appropriate environment for teaching the reading skills for each particular subject. This joint acceptance of responsibility will lead our students through a rewarding experience in the content courses, and teachers will receive professional satisfaction in observing youngsters as they enthusiastically meet the challenges of education.

References

Anderson, J. The readability of Australian newspapers. *Australian Journal of Psychology*, 1966, *18*, 80-83.

Baker, D. C., and MacDonald, J. C. Newspaper editorial readership and length of editorials. *Journalism Quarterly*, 1961, *38*, 473-79.

Brinton, J. E., and McKown, L. H. Effects of newspaper reading on knowledge and attitude. *Journalism Quarterly*, 1961, *38*, 187-95.

Carter, R. E., and Clarke, P. Suburbanites, city residents and local news. *Journalism Quarterly*, 1963, *40*, 548-58.

Danielson, W. A., and Bryan, S. D. Readability of wire stories in eight news categories. *Journalism Quarterly*, 1964, *41*, 105-06.

Dasbach, Anita Mallinckrodt. U. S.-Soviet magazine propaganda: *America Illustrated* and *USSR*. *Journalism Quarterly*, 1966, *43*, 73-84.

Deutschmann, P. J. *News-page content of twelve metropolitan dailies.* Cincinnati: Scripps-Howard Research, 1959.

Edelstein, A. S., and Larsen, O. N. The weekly press' contribution to a sense of urban community. *Journalism Quarterly*, 1960, *37*, 489-98.

Ellison, J., and Gosser, F. T. Non-fiction magazine articles: a content analysis study. *Journalism Quarterly*, 1959, *36*, 27-34.

Engel, G., O'Shea, Harriet E., and Mendenhall, J. H. "Projective" responses to a news article: a study in aspects of bias. *Journal of Psychology*, 1958, *46*, 309-17.

Gold, D., and Simmons, J. News selection patterns among Iowa dailies. *Public Opinion Quarterly*, 1965, *29*, 425-30.

Goldsmith, A. O. Comprehensibility of initials in headlines. *Journalism Quarterly*, 1958, *35*, 212-15.

Gregory, Margaret, and McLaughlin, W. J. Teaching the newspaper in junior high schools. *English Journal*, 1951, *40*, 23-28.

Griffin, P. F. Reader comprehension of news stories: a preliminary study. *Journalism Quarterly*, 1949, *26*, 389-96.

Haskins, J. B. Headline-and-lead scanning vs. whole-item reading in newspaper content analysis. *Journalism Quarterly*, 1966, *43*, 333-35.

Johnson, Lois V. Children's newspaper reading. *Elementary English*, 1963, *40*, 428-32, 444.

Lyle, J. Immediate vs. delayed reward use of newspapers by adolescents. *Journalism Quarterly*, 1962, *39*, 83-85.

Schramm, W., and Ludwig, M. The weekly newspaper and its readers. *Journalism Quarterly*, 1951, *28*, 301-14.

Sennett, T. B. The interpretive story as an aid to understanding news. *Journalism Quarterly*, 1954, *31*, 365-66.

Stempel, Guido H., III. Content patterns of small and metropolitan dailies. *Journalism Quarterly*, 1962, *39*, 88-90.

Stern, B. An analysis of readership of the daily newspaper "split" page. *Journalism Quarterly*, 1951, *28*, 225-28.

Stevenson, R. L. Readability of conservative and sensational papers since 1872. *Journalism Quarterly*, 1964, *41*, 201-06.

Stewart, Janice S. Content and readership of teen magazines. *Journalism Quarterly*, 1964, *41*, 580-83.

Swanson, C. E. What they read in 130 daily newspapers. *Journalism Quarterly*, 1955, *32*, 411-21.

Wilcox, W. Numbers and the news: graph, table or text? *Journalism Quarterly*, 1964, *41*, 38-44.

Other ERIC/CRIER + IRA Publications

The following ERIC/CRIER + IRA publications are available from the International Reading Association, Six Tyre Avenue, Newark, Delaware, 19711.

Bonnie Davis: *A guide to information sources for reading*

An annotated and directive compilation of potential sources in reading and related fields, available from IRA to members for $2.00 and to nonmembers for $2.50.

Edward G. Summers, Ed. *20 Year Annotated Index to* The Reading Teacher

Available from the International Reading Association for $3.00 to members of the Association and $3.50 to nonmembers. It is also available from EDRS (ED 031 608) in microfiche for $0.65.

Interpretive Papers

The following series was designed specifically to present research results in an easily readable style for special audiences. The papers are published by the International Reading Association and are available to members for $1.50 and to nonmembers for $2.00 from IRA. Microfiche is available from EDRS for $0.65.

Carl B. Smith, Barbara Carter, and Gloria Dapper: *Reading Problems and the Environment—the Principal's Role* (ED 024 847)

Carl B. Smith, Barbara Carter, and Gloria Dapper: *Establishing Central Reading Clinics—The Administrator's Role* (ED 024 849)

Carl B. Smith, Barbara Carter, and Gloria Dapper: *Treating Reading Disabilities—The Specialist's Role* (ED 024 850)

Carl B. Smith: *Correcting Reading Problems in the Classroom* (ED 024 848)

This paper is the first of a series analyzing discrete topics for specific audiences but offering useful information to anyone interested in the subject. Available from IRA for $1.00 to members and $1.50 to nonmembers. Microfiche is available from EDRS for $0.65.

Nicholas Anastasiow: *Oral language: expression of thought* (ED 054 393)

A series offering directive analyses of research on specific reading topics is available from IRA to members for $1.00 and to nonmembers for $1.50. Microfiche is available from EDRS for $0.65.

Eugene Jongsma: *The Cloze Procedure as a Teaching Technique* (ED 055 253)

MaryAnne Hall: *The Language Experience Approach for the Culturally Disadvantaged* (ED 058 468)

Diane Lapp: *Behavioral Objectives in Education*

These pamphlets are designed to answer parental questions on reading and are available from IRA in single copies or in quantity for prices as low as $0.20 each for 100 copies or more. Microfiche is available from EDRS for $0.65.

Rosemary Winebrenner: *How can I get my teenager to read?*

Norma Rogers: *What is reading readiness?*

Reading Research Profile Bibliographies

The following bibliographies are available to IRA members for $1.00, to nonmembers for $1.50. Microfiche is available from EDRS for $0.65.

Leo Fay: *Organization and Administration of School Reading Programs* (ED 046 677)

James L. Laffey: *Methods of Reading Instruction* (ED 047 930)

Roger Farr: *Measurement of Reading Achievement* (ED 049 906)

Leo Fay: *Reading Research: Methodology, Summaries, and Application* (ED 049 023)

Ordering Instructions

ERIC/CRIER+IRA publications can be ordered from the International Reading Association in paperback copy by citing the title and sending the amount listed to:

**International Reading Association
Six Tyre Avenue
Newark, Delaware 19711**

Microfiche reproductions of ERIC/CRIER+IRA publications are available from EDRS and can be obtained by writing:

**ERIC Document Reproduction Service
Leasco Information Products Company (LIPCO)
Post Office Drawer O
Bethesda, Maryland 20014**

This information must be furnished to order documents:

1] The accession number (ED number) of the desired document.
2] The type of reproduction desired—microfiche.
3] The number of copies being ordered.
4] The method of payment—cash with order, deposit, account, charge.
   a] The book rate or library rate postage is included in costs quoted.
   b] The difference between book rate or library rate and first class or foreign postage (outside continental United States) rate will be billed at cost.
   c] Payment must accompany orders totaling less than $10.00.
5] Standing orders for microfiche cost .089 cents per fiche, special collection cost is .14 per fiche, back collection cost is .089 per fiche.

EDRS will provide information on charges and deposit accounts upon request.

The Clearinghouses in the ERIC System

Adult Education
Syracuse University
Syracuse, New York 13210

Counseling and Personnel Services
Services Information Center
611 Church Street, 3d Floor
Ann Arbor, Michigan 48104

Early Childhood Education
University of Illinois
805 West Pennsylvania Avenue
Urbana, Illinois 61801

Educational Management
University of Oregon
Eugene, Oregon 97403

Educational Media and Technology
Institute for Communication Research
Cypress Hall
Stanford University
Palo Alto, California 94305

Exceptional Children
The Council for Exceptional Children
1499 Jefferson Davis Highway
Arlington, Virginia 22202

Higher Education
George Washington University
One Dupont Circle, Suite 630
Washington, D. C. 20036

Junior Colleges
Room 96, Powell Library
University of California
Los Angeles, California 90024

Languages and Linguistics
Modern Language Association of America (MLA)
62 Fifth Avenue
New York, New York 10011

Library and Information Sciences
American Society for Information Science
1140 Connecticut Ave., N.W., Suite 804
Washington, D. C. 20036

Reading
Indiana University
200 Pine Hall
Bloomington, Indiana 47401

Rural Education and Small Schools
Box AP
University Park Branch
New Mexico State University
Las Cruces, New Mexico 88001

Science Education
1460 West Lane Avenue
Columbus, Ohio 43221

Social Science Education
Academy Building
970 Aurora Avenue
Boulder, Colorado 80302

Teacher Education
One Dupont Circle, Suite 616
Washington, D. C. 20036

The Teaching of English
National Council of Teachers of English
508 South Sixth Street
Champaign, Illinois 61820

Tests, Measurements, and Evaluation
Educational Testing Service
Princeton, New Jersey 08540

Urban Disadvantaged
Teachers College
Columbia University
New York, New York 10027

Vocational and Technical Education
Ohio State University
1900 Kenny Road
Columbus, Ohio 43212